Applied Software Development
with Python & Machine
Learning by Wearable
& Wireless Systems for
Movement Disorder Treatment
via Deep Brain Stimulation

Applied Software Development with Python & Machine Learning by Wearable & Wireless Systems for Movement Disorder Treatment via Deep Brain Stimulation

Robert LeMoyne
Northern Arizona University, USA

Timothy Mastroianni

NEW JERSEY · LONDON · SINGAPORE · BEIJING · SHANGHAI · HONG KONG · TAIPEI · CHENNAI · TOKYO

Published by

World Scientific Publishing Co. Pte. Ltd.

5 Toh Tuck Link, Singapore 596224

USA office: 27 Warren Street, Suite 401-402, Hackensack, NJ 07601

UK office: 57 Shelton Street, Covent Garden, London WC2H 9HE

British Library Cataloguing-in-Publication Data
A catalogue record for this book is available from the British Library.

APPLIED SOFTWARE DEVELOPMENT WITH PYTHON & MACHINE LEARNING
BY WEARABLE & WIRELESS SYSTEMS FOR MOVEMENT DISORDER
TREATMENT VIA DEEP BRAIN STIMULATION

Copyright © 2022 by World Scientific Publishing Co. Pte. Ltd.

ISBN 978-981-123-595-5 (hardcover)
ISBN 978-981-123-596-2 (ebook for institutions)
ISBN 978-981-123-597-9 (ebook for individuals)

For any available supplementary material, please visit
https://www.worldscientific.com/worldscibooks/10.1142/12249#t=suppl

Typeset by Stallion Press
Email: enquiries@stallionpress.com

Printed in Singapore

Dedication

To my wife Mayumi, thank you for everything. Love Always.

I would like to thank my Mother, Father, and brother for their support.

"Nothing transcends the power of the human spirit."
from a homeless Vietnam Veteran and very loyal friend
And in the wind, he's still alive.

"To beat a tiger, one needs a brother's help."
Chinese Proverb
Thanks Tim.

Chiri mo tsumoreba yama to naru.
A favorite Japanese Proverb (in Romaji)
Translation:
Even dust piled up becomes a mountain.

I would like to thank my wife Mayumi for her kanji calligraphy skills for Figure 3.11.

I would also like to thank my coauthor Tim for his artistic skills for Figure 6.17.

We would like to extend our appreciation to Donald Whiting M.D. and Nestor Tomycz M.D. of Allegheny General Hospital for facilitating the opportunity to publish this endeavor.

Preface

The book presents the confluence of wearable and wireless inertial sensor systems, such as a smartphone, for deep brain stimulation for treating movement disorders, such as essential tremor, and machine learning. The machine learning distinguishes between distinct deep brain stimulation settings, such as 'On' and 'Off' status. This achievement demonstrates preliminary insight with respect to the concept of Network Centric Therapy, which essentially represents the Internet of Things for healthcare and the biomedical industry, inclusive of wearable and wireless inertial sensor systems, machine learning, and access to Cloud computing resources.

Imperative to the realization of these objectives is the organization of the software development process. Requirements and pseudo code are derived, and software automation using Python for post-processing the inertial sensor signal data to a feature set for machine learning is progressively developed. A perspective of machine learning in terms of a conceptual basis and operational overview is provided. Subsequently, an assortment of machine learning algorithms is evaluated based on the quantification of a reach and grasp task for essential tremor using a smartphone as a wearable and wireless accelerometer system.

Furthermore, these skills regarding the software development process and machine learning applications with wearable and wireless inertial sensor systems enable new and novel biomedical research only bounded by the reader's creativity.

Robert LeMoyne
Timothy Mastroianni

Contents

List of Figures

Chapter 1

Introduction

1.1 Introduction

During 2010, LeMoyne and Mastroianni sought to expand their research domain beyond the wireless accelerometer with local connectivity to a portable laptop computer. Their original configuration applied a wireless accelerometer that was effectively wearable for the quantification of reflex response and latency, gait, real-time feedback for gait, and the quantification of Parkinson's disease tremor [1–6]. The new extrapolation of the technology was the application of a smartphone as a wearable and wireless system for the quantification of Parkinson's disease hand tremor [7].

The discovery of the utility of the smartphone as a wearable and wireless inertial sensor system was evident as quantified signal data could be wirelessly transferred anywhere throughout the world for post-processing. This finding implies that the experimental location could be separated from the experimental site. Post-processing evolved from manual strategies to automated software and further expanded to the domain of machine learning classification to distinguish between human health status scenarios utilizing both the smartphone and portable media device [8–35].

One research subject of considerable interest originating from 2015 by LeMoyne and Mastroianni was the application of the smartphone to quantify essential tremor during a reach and grasp task with respect to deep brain stimulation set to 'On' and 'Off' status. During the post-processing of the accelerometer signal machine learning was applied to differentiate between the deep brain stimulation 'On' and 'Off' status [19]. This achievement of the smartphone has been applied for the quantification of essential tremor and Parkinson's disease as a wearable and wireless inertial sensor system. Machine learning was applied in conjunction to differentiate between deep brain stimulation set to 'On' and 'Off' status with considerable classification accuracy [13, 15, 19, 29–31, 33, 34].

This book intends to further advance the application of deep brain stimulation and machine learning with wearable and wireless inertial sensor systems, such as a smartphone, in the context of Network Centric Therapy for movement disorders, such as especially essential tremor. Similar applications are also pertinent to Parkinson's disease. A critical link for achieving the amalgamation of these technologies is the development of a robust software algorithm to provide automated post-processing of the acquired inertial sensor signal data to a consolidated feature set suitable for machine learning.

Python has been selected for developing the automated post-processing software. In order to achieve this task, a process for developing software is instilled that encompasses requirement definition, the development of pseudo code, incremental implementation of Python, preliminary testing and evaluation with anomaly resolution, and the evolution of the Python software to achieve robust automation of the consolidation of the inertial sensor signal data to a feature set for machine learning. The Waikato Environment for Knowledge Analysis (WEKA) is utilized for conducting the machine learning classification [36–38].

Seven machine learning algorithms through WEKA are evaluated in terms of their performance:

- J48 decision tree
- K-nearest neighbors
- Logistic regression
- Naïve Bayes
- Support vector machine
- Random forest
- Multilayer perceptron neural network

The approach for operating WEKA for these machine learning algorithms is thoroughly presented. Furthermore, a foundational perspective of the machine learning algorithms in terms of their strategies is discussed. This book incrementally develops an approach for achieving the objective of applying machine learning classification to distinguish deep brain stimulation set to 'On' and 'Off' status for a subject with essential tremor performing a reach and grasp task utilizing objectively quantified feedback acquired by the accelerometer signal of a smartphone as a wearable and wireless system with post-processing software automation using Python.

The objective of the book is achieved over the span of Chapter 2 through Chapter 7. Chapter 8 consists of relevant advanced concepts. A perspective of Chapter 2 through Chapter 8 is addressed.

1.2 Perspective of Chapter 2

Chapter 2, 'General Concept of Preliminary Network Centric Therapy Applying Deep Brain Stimulation for Ameliorating Movement Disorders with Machine Learning Classification using Python Based on Feedback from a Smartphone as a Wearable and Wireless System', establishes the foundation for proceeding to resolve the prescribed objective of the book. Movement disorders, such as essential tremor and Parkinson's disease, are elucidated in the context of their unique neuroanatomical origins, diagnosis, conventional therapy, and the advent of deep brain stimulation for highly specified therapy intervention, in light of numerous available parameter configurations [39–76]. The process of optimizing the deep brain stimulation system can present a laborious challenge [77–79]. Quantified feedback, such as through ordinal scales interpreted by a clinician, is controversial with respect to reliability [80–83].

In order to identify objective feedback for the response of a parameter configuration for deep brain stimulation, the wearable and wireless inertial sensor systems have been advocated for providing objectively quantified signal data [1–11, 13, 15–17, 19, 29–31, 33, 34, 50, 75, 76, 84–87]. Wearable and wireless inertial sensor systems have been instilled for the evaluation of movement disorders and intervention efficacy [88–94]. During 2010, LeMoyne *et al.* utilized a software application for a smartphone known as Vibration, developed by Diffraction Limited Design LLC, for quantifying Parkinson's disease hand tremor with wireless connectivity to the Internet [7, 95].

This software application is available for the iPhone (a smartphone) and associated iPod (a portable media device), which currently can obtain accelerometer and gyroscope signal data for the evaluation of human health status [6–29, 32, 35, 87]. The acquired inertial sensor signal data can be incorporated into a feature set for machine learning, which has been demonstrated for the distinction of human health status and the determination of deep brain stimulation efficacy [9–35, 84, 85, 87, 96–98]. WEKA enables the basis for these machine learning classification endeavors, and the inertial sensor signal data is consolidated into an Attribute-Relation File Format (ARFF), which signifies the relevance of automated post-processing software [9–38, 84, 85, 87, 96–98].

1.3 Perspective of Chapter 3

Chapter 3, 'Global Algorithm Development', provides an organized and definitive process for developing the software algorithm for realizing automated post-processing software. The multiple software development processes, such as with respect to the waterfall model and incremental development, are addressed that inherently utilize the establishment of requirements to achieve the prescribed software objectives [99, 100]. The development of requirements is imperative for software applied to regulated environments, such as for medical applications [101]. The Fagan inspection techniques provides the opportunity to enhance the clarity and impact of the requirements [102, 103].

The subsequent phases involve design, implementation, and testing of the software, for which pseudo code further details the intent of the requirements that are suitable for machine learning classification through WEKA [36–38, 104–106]. Another aspect of the software development process pertains to the selection of an appropriate programming language with consideration applied to Python, R, and

Octave [107–110]. The selection of Python enables the Anaconda Distribution and Jupyter Notebook to be designated as the software development platform [111, 112]. Appropriate Python libraries can be determined, and resources for implementing Python programming syntax are consulted [107, 108, 113–119]. During the software development process terminal phases, Kaizen, symbolizing continuous improvement in Japanese, can be incorporated [120, 121].

1.4 Perspective of Chapter 4

Chapter 4, 'Incremental Software Development using Python', evolves the software development process from the previously established requirements and pseudo code [99, 100]. Python, which is the software language that facilitates the implementation of the requirements, is incrementally implemented for visualizing the accelerometer signal for the essential tremor reach and grasp task with the deep brain stimulation set to 'On' mode [108, 116, 122]. With this single instance of trial data, the accelerometer signal is post-processed to a preliminary ARFF file, which is the established from previous successful machine learning classification applications using WEKA that incorporate software automation to consolidate signal data, such as from an inertial sensor, to a numeric attribute derived feature set [9–38, 84, 85, 87, 96–98, 123–126].

Realizing the software program represents the next phase of the software development process [104]. Requirements and pseudo code are converted to Python syntax [99, 100, 108, 116, 122, 127]. Subsequently, testing and evaluation of the preliminary software is incorporated, which ascertains an anomaly in the accelerometer signal that enables further resolution for the more robust acquisition of the feature set [105].

1.5 Perspective of Chapter 5

Chapter 5, 'Automation of Feature Set Extraction using Python', presents the development of automated post-processing based on the previous preliminary post-processing software accomplished in Chapter 4, 'Incremental Software Development using Python'. The foundation of this next phase of software development is the evolved require-ments, pseudo code, and associated Kaizen techniques, for which this phase of software development process incorporates amendable Python syntax to realize the requirements [99, 100, 104, 120, 121, 128–132]. Preliminary phase of the development software automation illustrates the accelerometer signal for the essential tremor reach and grasp task using the smartphone as a wearable and wireless system with the deep brain stimulation system using the 'On' mode [19]. Software reuse is applied for the correlated experiment incorporating the deep brain stimulation system using the 'Off' mode [19, 133, 134]. The convergence of the software development process achieves automated consolidation of the accelerometer signal to an ARFF file appropriate for WEKA through Python in a manner that has been previously rec-ommended and applied [9–38, 84, 85, 87, 96–98, 123–126].

1.6 Perspective of Chapter 6

Chapter 6, 'Waikato Environment for Knowledge Analysis (WEKA) a Perspective Consideration of Multiple Machine Learning Classification Algorithms and Applications', involves the application of machine learning for classifying the disparate scenarios of the essential tremor reach and grasp task with respect to the deep brain stimulation system set to 'On' and 'Off' status. The inertial sensor data is acquired using the smartphone as a wearable and wireless system for quantifying tremor [19]. Python facilitates the automated post-processing of the acquired inertial sensor signal using the smartphone to an ARFF file suitable for WEKA. The post-processing technique is in conjunction with previously advocated and implemented strategies for the applica-tion of machine learning incorporating wearable and wireless systems [9–38, 84, 85, 87, 96–98, 123–126]. Seven machine learning algo-rithms (J48 decision tree, K-nearest neighbors, logistic regression, naïve Bayes, support vector machine, random forest, and multilayer perceptron neural network) available through WEKA are comprehen-sively described in terms of their fundamental algorithms and demon-strated in terms of their operation with the use of tenfold cross-validation [36–38, 135–162].

1.7 Perspective of Chapter 7

Chapter 7, 'Machine Learning Classification of Essential Tremor using a Reach and Grasp Task with Deep Brain Stimulation System Set to 'On' and 'Off' Status' presents the assessment of WEKA that has been established by precedence through multiple previous applications involving wearable and wireless inertial sensor systems for differentiating between health status scenarios through machine learning [9–38, 84, 85, 87, 96–98, 123–126]. The seven machine learning algorithms provided by WEKA, as mentioned in the previous section, are considered. With respect to the resultant machine learning models developed, classification accuracy is the most significant performance parameter. With respect to machine learning models that do not attain 100% classification accuracy, confusion matrix is a subject of consideration. An additionally important parameter, which is the time to develop the machine learning model, is addressed. In summary, a detailed perspective of the efficacy for machine learning classification with regards to deep brain stimulation system set to 'On' and 'Off' status using a smartphone functioning as a wearable and wireless inertial sensor for quantifying the essential tremor reach and grasp task is presented.

1.8 Perspective of Chapter 8

Chapter 8, 'Advanced Concepts', discusses future applications that are anticipated to have considerable impact, such as Network Centric Therapy. Network Centric Therapy represents the application of wearable and wireless inertial sensor systems for healthcare, such as with respect to movement disorders, with Cloud computing access and machine learning for augmented clinical acuity [13, 16, 17, 47]. Recent developments incorporate conformal wearable and wireless inertial sensor systems for distinguishing an assortment of deep brain stimulation parameter configurations for treating movement disorders through the application of machine learning [17, 84, 85, 163, 164]. Additionally, these techniques have been extended to the domain of deep learning [165, 166].

1.9 Conclusion

In summary, the book presents as thoroughly defined methodology for achieving the prescribed objective of incorporating machine learning classification to differentiate deep brain stimulation set to 'On' and 'Off' status for a subject with essential tremor conducting a reach and grasp task that is quantified by the accelerometer signal of a smartphone constituting a wearable and wireless system. Post-processing software automation is achieved through Python. WEKA enables an assortment of machine learning algorithms, such as the J48 decision tree, K-nearest neighbors, logistic regression, naïve Bayes, support vector machine, random forest, and multilayer perceptron neural network. These machine learning algorithms are contrasted with respect to classification accuracy and time to develop the machine learning model.

In order to accomplish the prescribed objective, essential tremor with the associated reach and grasp task is discussed, and the opportunity to quantify this task through a smartphone as a wearable and wireless accelerometer system is presented. In order to apply the acquired accelerometer signal data for machine learning classification using WEKA, automation software is imperative for consolidating the accelerometer signal data to a feature set. The software development process is applied with global algorithm development of requirements and pseudo code. Python is progressively and incrementally applied to achieve automated post-processing of the accelerometer signal data for machine learning application. The J48 decision tree, K-nearest neighbors, logistic regression, naïve Bayes, support vector machine, random forest, and multilayer perceptron neural network are available through WEKA, and a perspective of their algorithms and operation using WEKA is discussed. The ability of these machine learning techniques to differentiate between deep brain stimulation set to 'On' and 'Off' status for a subject with essential tremor conducting a reach and grasp task is evaluated in terms of classification accuracy and time to develop the machine learning model. Additionally, advanced concepts anticipated to significantly evolve Network Centric Therapy, such as conformal wearable and wireless systems and deep learning, are addressed.

References

1. LeMoyne, R., Coroian, C., Mastroianni, T., Opalinski, P., Cozza, M. and Grundfest W. (2009). *Biomedical Engineering*, ed. Barros de Mello, C. A., Chapter 10 "The Merits of Artificial Proprioception, with Applications in Biofeedback Gait Rehabilitation Concepts and Movement Disorder Characterization," (InTech, Vienna) pp. 165–198.

2. LeMoyne, R. (2007). Gradient optimized neuromodulation for Parkinson's disease, *Proc. 12th Annual UCLA Research Conference on Aging*.

3. LeMoyne, R., Coroian, C. and Mastroianni, T. (2008). 3D wireless accelerometer characterization of Parkinson's disease status, *Proc. Plasticity and Repair in Neurodegenerative Disorders*.

4. LeMoyne, R., Coroian, C. and Mastroianni, T. (2009). Quantification of Parkinson's disease characteristics using wireless accelerometers, *Proc. ICME International Conference on IEEE Complex Medical Engineering (CME)*, pp. 1–5.

5. LeMoyne, R., Mastroianni, T. and Grundfest, W. (2013). Wireless accelerometer configuration for monitoring Parkinson's disease hand tremor, *Adv. Park. Dis.*, 2, pp. 62–67.

6. LeMoyne, R. (2013). Wearable and wireless accelerometer systems for monitoring Parkinson's disease patients-a perspective review, *Adv. Park. Dis.*, 2, pp. 113–115.

7. LeMoyne, R., Mastroianni, T., Cozza, M., Coroian, C. and Grundfest, W. (2010). Implementation of an iPhone for characterizing Parkinson's disease tremor through a wireless accelerometer application, *Proc. 32nd Annual International Conference of the IEEE, Engineering in Medicine and Biology Society (EMBS)*, pp. 4954–4958.

8. LeMoyne, R. and Mastroianni, T. (2015). *Mobile Health Technologies, Methods and Protocols*, eds. Rasooly, A. and Herold, K. E., Chapter 23 "Use of Smartphones and Portable Media Devices for Quantifying Human Movement Characteristics of Gait, Tendon Reflex Response, and Parkinson's Disease Hand Tremor," (Springer, New York) pp. 335–358.

9. LeMoyne, R. and Mastroianni, T. (2016). *Telemedicine*, "Telemedicine Perspectives for Wearable and Wireless Applications Serving the

Domain of Neurorehabilitation and Movement Disorder Treatment," (SM Group, Dover, Delaware) pp. 1–10.

10. LeMoyne, R. and Mastroianni, T. (2017). *Wireless MEMS Networks and Applications*, ed. Uttamchandani, D., Chapter 6 "Wearable and Wireless Gait Analysis Platforms: Smartphones and Portable Media Devices," (Elsevier, New York) pp. 129–152.

11. LeMoyne, R. and Mastroianni, T. (2017). *Smartphones from an Applied Research Perspective*, ed. Mohamudally, N., Chapter 1 "Smartphone and Portable Media Device: A Novel Pathway Toward the Diagnostic Characterization of Human Movement," (InTech, Rijeka, Croatia) pp. 1–24.

12. LeMoyne, R. and Mastroianni, T. (2018). *Wearable and Wireless Systems for Healthcare I: Gait and Reflex Response Quantification*, (Springer, Singapore).

13. LeMoyne, R., Mastroianni, T., Whiting, D. and Tomycz, N. (2019). *Wearable and Wireless Systems for Healthcare II: Movement Disorder Evaluation and Deep Brain Stimulation Systems*, (Springer, Singapore).

14. LeMoyne, R. and Mastroianni, T. (2018). *Wearable and Wireless Systems for Healthcare I: Gait and Reflex Response Quantification*, Chapter 9 "Role of Machine Learning for Gait and Reflex Response Classification," (Springer, Singapore) pp. 111–120.

15. LeMoyne, R., Mastroianni, T., Whiting, D. and Tomycz, N. (2019). *Wearable and Wireless Systems for Healthcare II: Movement Disorder Evaluation and Deep Brain Stimulation Systems*, Chapter 8 "Role of Machine Learning for Classification of Movement Disorder and Deep Brain Stimulation Status," (Springer, Singapore) pp. 99–111.

16. LeMoyne, R. and Mastroianni, T. (2019). *Smartphones: Recent Innovations and Applications*, ed. Dabove, P., Chapter 7 "Network Centric Therapy for Wearable and Wireless Systems," (Nova Science Publishers, Hauppauge).

17. LeMoyne, R. and Mastroianni, T. (2020). *Multilayer Perceptrons: Theory and Applications*, ed. Vang-Mata, R., Chapter 2 "Machine Learning Classification for Network Centric Therapy Utilizing the Multilayer Perceptron Neural Network," (Nova Science Publishers, Hauppauge) pp. 39–76.

18. LeMoyne, R., Kerr, W., Zanjani, K. and Mastroianni, T. (2014). Implementation of an iPod wireless accelerometer application using machine learning to classify disparity of hemiplegic and healthy patellar tendon reflex pair, *J. Med. Imaging Health Inform.*, 4, pp. 21–28.

19. LeMoyne, R., Tomycz, N., Mastroianni, T., McCandless, C., Cozza, M. and Peduto, D. (2015). Implementation of a smartphone wireless accelerometer platform for establishing deep brain stimulation treatment efficacy of essential tremor with machine learning, *Proc. 37th Annual International Conference of the IEEE, Engineering in Medicine and Biology Society (EMBS)*, pp. 6772–6775.

20. LeMoyne, R. and Mastroianni, T. (2015). Machine learning classification of a hemiplegic and healthy patellar tendon reflex pair through an iPod wireless gyroscope platform, *Proc. 45th Society for Neuroscience Annual Meeting*.

21. LeMoyne, R., Kerr, W. and Mastroianni, T. (2015). Implementation of machine learning with an iPod application mounted to cane for classifying assistive device usage, *J. Med. Imaging Health Inform.*, 5, pp. 1404–1408.

22. LeMoyne, R., Mastroianni, T., Hessel, A. and Nishikawa, K. (2015). Ankle rehabilitation system with feedback from a smartphone wireless gyroscope platform and machine learning classification, *Proc. 14th International Conference on Machine Learning and Applications (ICMLA), IEEE*, pp. 406–409.

23. LeMoyne, R. and Mastroianni, T. (2016). Implementation of a smartphone as a wireless gyroscope platform for quantifying reduced arm swing in hemiplegic gait with machine learning classification by multilayer perceptron neural network, *Proc. 38th Annual International Conference of the IEEE, Engineering in Medicine and Biology Society (EMBS)*, pp. 2626–2630.

24. LeMoyne, R. and Mastroianni, T. (2016). Smartphone wireless gyroscope platform for machine learning classification of hemiplegic patellar tendon reflex pair disparity through a multilayer perceptron neural network, *Proc. Wireless Health (WH), IEEE*, pp. 1–6.

25. LeMoyne, R. and Mastroianni, T. (2016). Implementation of a multilayer perceptron neural network for classifying a hemiplegic and

healthy reflex pair using an iPod wireless gyroscope platform, *Proc. 46th Society for Neuroscience Annual Meeting.*

26. LeMoyne, R. and Mastroianni, T. (2017). Virtual proprioception for eccentric training, *Proc. 39th Annual International Conference of the IEEE, Engineering in Medicine and Biology Society (EMBS),* pp. 4557–4561.

27. LeMoyne, R. and Mastroianni, T. (2017). Wireless gyroscope platform enabled by a portable media device for quantifying wobble board therapy, *Proc. 39th Annual International Conference of the IEEE, Engineering in Medicine and Biology Society (EMBS),* pp. 2662–2666.

28. LeMoyne, R. and Mastroianni, T. (2017). Implementation of a smartphone wireless gyroscope platform with machine learning for classifying disparity of a hemiplegic patellar tendon reflex pair, *J. Mech. Med. Biol.,* 17, 1750083.

29. LeMoyne, R., Mastroianni, T., Tomycz, N., Whiting, D., Oh, M., McCandless, C., Currivan, C. and Peduto, D. (2017). Implementation of a multilayer perceptron neural network for classifying deep brain stimulation in 'On' and 'Off' modes through a smartphone representing a wearable and wireless sensor application, *Proc. 47th Society for Neuroscience Annual Meeting, Featured in Hot Topics (Top 1% of Abstracts).*

30. LeMoyne, R., Mastroianni, T., McCandless, C., Currivan, C., Whiting, D. and Tomycz, N. (2018). Implementation of a smartphone as a wearable and wireless accelerometer and gyroscope platform for ascertaining deep brain stimulation treatment efficacy of Parkinson's disease through machine learning classification, *Adv. Park. Dis.,* 7, pp. 19–30.

31. LeMoyne, R., Mastroianni, T., McCandless, C., Currivan, C., Whiting, D. and Tomycz, N. (2018). Implementation of a smartphone as a wearable and wireless inertial sensor platform for determining efficacy of deep brain stimulation for Parkinson's disease tremor through machine learning, *Proc. 48th Society for Neuroscience Annual Meeting, Nanosymposium.*

32. LeMoyne, R. and Mastroianni, T. (2018). Implementation of a smartphone as a wearable and wireless gyroscope platform for machine learning classification of hemiplegic gait through a multilayer

perceptron neural network, *Proc. 17th International Conference on Machine Learning and Applications (ICMLA), IEEE*, pp. 946–950.

33. LeMoyne, R., Mastroianni, T., Whiting, D. and Tomycz, N. (2019). *Wearable and Wireless Systems for Healthcare II: Movement Disorder Evaluation and Deep Brain Stimulation Systems*, Chapter 9 "Assessment of Machine Learning Classification Strategies for the Differentiation of Deep Brain Stimulation "On" and "Off" Status for Parkinson's Disease Using a Smartphone as a Wearable and Wireless Inertial Sensor for Quantified Feedback," (Springer, Singapore) pp. 113–126.

34. LeMoyne, R., Mastroianni, T., McCandless, C., Whiting, D. and Tomycz, N. (2019). Evaluation of machine learning algorithms for classifying deep brain stimulation respective of 'On' and 'Off' status, *Proc. 9th International IEEE Conference on Neural Engineering (NER), IEEE/EMBS*, pp. 483–488.

35. Mastroianni, T. and LeMoyne, R. (2016). Application of a multilayer perceptron neural network with an iPod as a wireless gyroscope platform to classify reduced arm swing gait for people with Erb's palsy, *Proc. 46th Society for Neuroscience Annual Meeting*.

36. Hall, M., Frank, E., Holmes, G., Pfahringer, B., Reutemann, P. and Witten I. H. (2009). The WEKA data mining software: An update, *ACM SIGKDD Explor. Newsl.*, 11, pp. 10–18.

37. Witten, I. H., Frank, E. and Hall, M. A. (2011). *Data Mining: Practical Machine Learning Tools and Techniques*, 3rd Ed. (Morgan Kaufmann Publishers, Burlington).

38. WEKA [www.cs.waikato.ac.nz/~ml/weka]

39. Parkinson, J. (1817). *An Essay on the Shaking Palsy*, (Whittingham and Rowland, London).

40. Louis, E. D. (2005). Essential tremor, *Lancet Neurol.*, 4, pp. 100–110.

41. Louis, E. D. (2000). Essential tremor, *Arch. Neurol. (JAMA Neurol.)*, 57, pp. 1522–1524.

42. Kandel, E. R., Schwartz, J. H. and Jessell, T. M. (2000). *Principles of Neural Science*, 4th Ed., Chapter 43 "The Basal Ganglia," (McGraw-Hill, New York) pp. 853–867.

43. Essential Tremor [www.essentialtremor.org]

44. Seeley, R. R., Stephens, T. D. and Tate, P. (2003). *Anatomy and Physiology*, 6th Ed., Chapter 14 "Integration of Nervous System Functions," (McGraw-Hill, Boston,) pp. 465–500.

45. Deuschl, G., Raethjen, J., Hellriegel, H. and Elble, R. (2011). Treatment of patients with essential tremor, *Lancet Neurol.*, 10, pp. 148–161.

46. Habib-ur-Rehman. (2000). Diagnosis and management of tremor, *Arch. Intern. Med.*, 160, pp. 2438–2444.

47. LeMoyne, R., Mastroianni, T., Whiting, D. and Tomycz, N. (2019). *Wearable and Wireless Systems for Healthcare II: Movement Disorder Evaluation and Deep Brain Stimulation Systems*, Chapter 1 "Wearable and Wireless Systems for Movement Disorder Evaluation and Deep Brain Stimulation Systems," (Springer, Singapore) pp. 1–15.

48. Nolte, J. and Sundsten, J. W. (2002). *The Human Brain: An Introduction to its Functional Anatomy*, 5th Ed., Chapter 19 "Basal Ganglia," (Mosby, St. Louis) pp. 464–485.

49. Williams, R. (2010). Alim-Louis Benabid: Stimulation and serendipity, *Lancet Neurol.*, 9, pp. 1152.

50. Amon, A. and Alesch, F. (2017). Systems for deep brain stimulation: Review of technical features, *J. Neural. Transm.*, 124, pp. 1083–1091.

51. Bickley, L. S. and Szilagyi, P. G. (2003). *Bates' Guide to Physical Examination and History Taking*, 8th Ed., Chapter 17 "The Nervous System," (Lippincott Williams and Wilkins, Philadelphia) pp. 681–764.

52. Ramaker, C., Marinus, J., Stiggelbout, A. M. and Van Hilten, B. J. (2002). Systematic evaluation of rating scales for impairment and disability in Parkinson's disease, *Mov. Disord.*, 17, pp. 867–876.

53. Fahn, S., Elton, R. and UPDRS Development Committee. (1987). *Recent Developments in Parkinson's Disease, Vol. 2.*, eds. Fahn, S., Marsden, C. D., Calne, D. B. and Goldstein, M., "Unified Parkinson's Disease Rating Scale," (Macmillan Health Care Information, Florham Park) pp. 153–163, 293–304.

54. Goetz, C. G., Stebbins, G. T., Chmura, T. A., Fahn, S., Poewe, W. and Tanner, C. M. (2010). Teaching program for the Movement Disorder Society-sponsored revision of the Unified Parkinson's Disease Rating Scale: (MDS-UPDRS), *Mov. Disord.*, 25, pp. 1190–1194.

55. Movement Disorder Society Task Force on Rating Scales for Parkinson's Disease. (2003). The Unified Parkinson's Disease Rating Scale (UPDRS): Status and recommendations, *Mov. Disord.*, 18, pp. 738–750.

56. Goetz, C. G., Tilley, B. C., Shaftman, S. R., Stebbins, G. T., Fahn, S., Martinez-Martin, P., Poewe, W., Sampaio, C., Stern, M. B., Dodel, R., Dubois, B., Holloway, R., Jankovic, J., Kulisevsky, J., Lang, A. E., Lees, A., Leurgans, S., LeWitt, P. A., Nyenhuis, D., Olanow, C. W., Rascol, O., Schrag, A., Teresi, J. A., van Hilten, J. J. and LaPelle, N. (2008). Movement Disorder Society-sponsored revision of the Unified Parkinson's Disease Rating Scale (MDS-UPDRS): Scale presentation and clinimetric testing results, *Mov. Disord.*, 23, pp. 2129–2170.

57. Fahn, S., Tolosa, E. and Marin, C. (1988). *Parkinson's Disease and Movement Disorders*, Chapter 17 "Clinical Rating Scale for Tremor," (Urban & Schwarzenberg, Baltimore) pp. 225–234.

58. Elble, R. J. (2016). The essential tremor rating assessment scale, *J. Neurol. Neuromed.*, 1, pp. 34–38.

59. LeMoyne, R., Mastroianni, T., Whiting, D. and Tomycz, N. (2019). *Wearable and Wireless Systems for Healthcare II: Movement Disorder Evaluation and Deep Brain Stimulation Systems*, Chapter 2 "Movement Disorders: Parkinson's Disease and Essential Tremor — A General Perspective," (Springer, Singapore) pp. 17–24.

60. Hossen, A., Muthuraman, M., Al-Hakim, Z., Raethjen, J., Deuschl, G. and Heute, U. (2013). Discrimination of Parkinsonian tremor from essential tremor using statistical signal characterization of the spectrum of accelerometer signal, *Biomed. Mater. Eng.*, 23, pp. 513–531.

61. Diamond, M. C., Scheibel, A. B. and Elson, L. M. (1985). *The Human Brain Coloring Book*, Chapter 5 "Introduction: The Brain," (Harper Perennial, New York) pp. 5–24, 5–25.

62. Paris-Robidas, S., Brochu, E., Sintes, M., Emond, V., Bousquet, M., Vandal, M., Pilote, M., Tremblay, C., Di Paolo, T., Rajput, A. H., Rajput, A. and Calon, F. (2012). Defective dentate nucleus GABA receptors in essential tremor, *Brain*, 135, pp. 105–116.

63. The Parkinson Study Group. (2004). Levodopa and the progression of Parkinson's disease, *N. Engl. J. Med.*, 351, pp. 2498–2508.

64. Giller, C. A., Dewey, R. B., Ginsburg, M.I., Mendelsohn, D. B. and Berk, A. M. (1998). Stereotactic pallidotomy and thalamotomy using individual variations of anatomic landmarks for localization, *Neurosurgery*, 42, pp. 56–65.

65. Niranjan, A., Kondziolka, D., Baser, S., Heyman, R. and Lunsford, L. D. (2000). Functional outcomes after gamma knife thalamotomy for essential tremor and MS-related tremor, *Neurology*, 55, pp. 443–446.

66. Young, R. F., Jacques, S., Mark, R., Kopyov, O., Copcutt, B., Posewitz, A. and Li, F. (2000). Gamma knife thalamotomy for treatment of tremor: Long-term results, *J. Neurosurg.*, 93, pp. 128–135.

67. Flora, E. D., Perera, C. L., Cameron, A. L. and Maddern, G.J. (2010). Deep brain stimulation for essential tremor: A systematic review, *Mov. Disord.*, 25, pp. 1550–1559.

68. Miocinovic, S., Somayajula, S., Chitnis, S. and Vitek, J. L. (2013). History, applications, and mechanisms of deep brain stimulation, *JAMA Neurol.*, 70, pp. 163–171.

69. Benabid, A. L., Pollak, P., Louveau, A., Henry, S. and de Rougemont, J. (1987). Combined (thalamotomy and stimulation) stereotactic surgery of the VIM thalamic nucleus for bilateral Parkinson's disease, *Appl. Neurophysiol.*, 50, pp. 344–346.

70. Yu, H. and Neimat, J. S. (2008). The treatment of movement disorders by deep brain stimulation, *Neurotherapeutics*, 5, pp. 26–36.

71. LeMoyne, R., Mastroianni, T., Whiting, D. and Tomycz, N. (2019). *Wearable and Wireless Systems for Healthcare II: Movement Disorder Evaluation and Deep Brain Stimulation Systems*, Chapter 4 "Deep Brain Stimulation for the Treatment of Movement Disorder Regarding Parkinson's Disease and Essential Tremor with Device Characterization," (Springer, Singapore) pp. 37–51.

72. Hassler, R. (1959). Introduction to Stereotaxis with an Atlas of the Human Brain, eds. Schaltenbrand G. and Bailey P. "Anatomy of the Thalamus," (Thieme, Stuttgart) pp. 230–290.

73. LeMoyne, R., Mastroianni, T., Whiting, D. and Tomycz, N. (2019). *Wearable and Wireless Systems for Healthcare II: Movement Disorder Evaluation and Deep Brain Stimulation Systems*, Chapter 5 "Surgical Procedure for Deep Brain Stimulation Implantation

and Operative Phase with Postoperative Risks," (Springer, Singapore) pp. 53–63.

74. Constantoyannis, C., Berk, C., Honey, C. R., Mendez, I. and Brownstone, R. M. (2005). Reducing hardware-related complications of deep brain stimulation, *Can. J. Neurol. Sci.*, 32, pp. 194–200.

75. Volkmann, J., Moro, E. and Pahwa, R. (2006). Basic algorithms for the programming of deep brain stimulation in Parkinson's disease, *Mov. Disord.*, 21, pp. S284–S289.

76. Isaias, I. U. and Tagliati, M. (2008). *Deep Brain Stimulation in Neurological and Psychiatric Disorders*, eds. Tarsy, D., Vitek, J. L., Starr, P. A. and Okun, M. S., Chapter 20 "Deep Brain Stimulation Programming for Movement Disorders," (Springer, New York) pp. 361–397.

77. Pretto, T. (2007). Deep brain stimulation, *Neurologist*, 13, pp. 103–104.

78. Butson, C. R. and McIntyre, C. C. (2008). Current steering to control the volume of tissue activated during deep brain stimulation, *Brain Stimul.*, 1, pp. 7–15.

79. Panisset, M., Picillo, M., Jodoin, N., Poon, Y. Y., Valencia-Mizrachi, A., Fasano, A., Munhoz, R. and Honey, C. R. (2017). Establishing a standard of care for deep brain stimulation centers in Canada, *Can. J. Neurol. Sci.*, 44, pp. 132–138.

80. Siderowf, A., McDermott, M., Kieburtz, K., Blindauer, K., Plumb, S. and Shoulson, I. (2002). Test-retest reliability of the unified Parkinson's disease rating scale in patients with early Parkinson's disease: Results from a multicenter clinical trial, *Mov. Disord.*, 17, pp. 758–763.

81. Metman, L. V., Myre, B., Verwey, N., Hassin-Baer, S., Arzbaecher, J., Sierens, D. and Bakay, R. (2004). Test-retest reliability of UPDRS-III, dyskinesia scales, and timed motor tests in patients with advanced Parkinson's disease: An argument against multiple baseline assessments, *Mov. Disord.*, 19, pp. 1079–1084.

82. Richards, M., Marder, K., Cote, L. and Mayeux, R. (1994). Interrater reliability of the unified parkinson's disease rating scale motor examination, *Mov. Disord.*, 9, pp. 89–91.

83. Post, B., Merkus, M. P., de Bie, R. M., de Haan, R. J. and Speelman, J. D. (2005). Unified parkinson's disease rating Scale motor examination:

Are ratings of nurses, residents in neurology, and movement disorders specialists interchangeable?, *Mov. Disord.*, 20, pp. 1577–1584.

84. LeMoyne, R., Mastroianni, T., Whiting, D. and Tomycz, N. (2019). Network Centric Therapy for deep brain stimulation status parametric analysis with machine learning classification, *Proc. 49th Society for Neuroscience Annual Meeting, Nanosymposium.*

85. LeMoyne, R., Mastroianni, T., Whiting, D. and Tomycz, N. (2019). Preliminary Network Centric Therapy for machine learning classification of deep brain stimulation status for the treatment of Parkinson's disease with a conformal wearable and wireless inertial sensor, *Adv. Park. Dis.*, 8, pp. 75–91.

86. LeMoyne, R., Mastroianni, T., Whiting, D. and Tomycz, N. (2019). *Wearable and Wireless Systems for Healthcare II: Movement Disorder Evaluation and Deep Brain Stimulation Systems,* Chapter 6 "Preliminary Wearable and Locally Wireless Systems for Quantification of Parkinson's Disease and Essential Tremor Characteristics," (Springer, Singapore) pp. 65–78.

87. LeMoyne, R., Mastroianni, T., Whiting, D. and Tomycz, N. (2019). *Wearable and Wireless Systems for Healthcare II: Movement Disorder Evaluation and Deep Brain Stimulation Systems,* Chapter 7 "Wearable and Wireless Systems with Internet Connectivity for Quantification of Parkinson's Disease and Essential Tremor Characteristics," (Springer, Singapore) pp. 79–97.

88. Schrag, A., Schelosky, L., Scholz, U. and Poewe, W. (1999). Reduction of parkinsonian signs in patients with Parkinson's disease by dopaminergic versus anticholinergic single-dose challenges, *Mov. Disord.*, 14, pp. 252–255.

89. Keijsers, N. L., Horstink, M. W., van Hilten, J. J., Hoff, J. I. and Gielen, C. C. (2000). Detection and assessment of the severity of levodopa-induced dyskinesia in patients with Parkinson's disease by neural networks, *Mov. Disord.*, 15, pp. 1104–1111.

90. Keijsers, N. L., Horstink, M. W. and Gielen, S. C. (2006). Ambulatory motor assessment in Parkinson's disease, *Mov. Disord.*, 21, pp. 34–44.

91. Gurevich, T. Y., Shabtai, H., Korczyn, A. D., Simon, E. S. and Giladi, N. (2006). Effect of rivastigmine on tremor in patients with Parkinson's disease and dementia, *Mov. Disord.*, 21, pp. 1663–1666.

92. Obwegeser, A. A., Uitti, R. J., Witte, R. J., Lucas, J. A., Turk, M. F. and Wharen, R. E. Jr. (2001). Quantitative and qualitative outcome measures after thalamic deep brain stimulation to treat disabling tremors, *Neurosurgery*, 48, pp. 274–284.

93. Kumru, H., Summerfield, C., Valldeoriola, F. and Valls-Solé, J. (2004). Effects of subthalamic nucleus stimulation on characteristics of EMG activity underlying reaction time in Parkinson's disease, *Mov. Disord.*, 19, pp. 94–100.

94. Giuffrida, J. P., Riley, D. E., Maddux, B. N. and Heldman, D. A. (2009). Clinically deployable Kinesia™ technology for automated tremor assessment, *Mov. Disord.*, 24, pp. 723–730.

95. Diffraction Limited Design LLC [www.dld-llc.com/Diffraction_Limited_Design_LLC/Vibration.html]

96. LeMoyne, R., Heerinckx, F., Aranca, T., De Jager, R., Zesiewicz, T. and Saal, H. J. (2016). Wearable body and wireless inertial sensors for machine learning classification of gait for people with Friedreich's ataxia, *Proc. 13th Annual International Body Sensor Networks Conference (BSN), IEEE*, pp. 147–151.

97. LeMoyne, R. and Mastroianni, T. (2018). *Wearable and Wireless Systems for Healthcare I: Gait and Reflex Response Quantification*, Chapter 6 "Smartphones and Portable Media Devices as Wearable and Wireless Systems for Gait and Reflex Response Quantification," (Springer, Singapore) pp. 73–93.

98. LeMoyne, R. and Mastroianni, T. (2018). *Wearable and Wireless Systems for Healthcare I: Gait and Reflex Response Quantification*, Chapter 10 "Homebound Therapy with Wearable and Wireless Systems," (Springer, Singapore) pp. 121–132.

99. Sommerville, I. (2011). *Software Engineering*, 9th Ed., Chapter 2 "Software Processes," (Addison Wesley, New York) pp. 27–55.

100. Sommerville, I. (2011). *Software Engineering*, 9th Ed., Chapter 4 "Requirements Engineering," (Addison Wesley, New York) pp. 82–117.

101. Food and Drug Administration. (2002). *General Principles of Software Validation; Final Guidance for Industry and FDA Staff*, (Food and Drug Administration, Rockville).

102. Fagan, M. E. (1986). Advances in software inspections, *IEEE Trans. Softw. Eng.*, SE-12, pp. 744–751.

103. Fagan, M. E. (1999). Design and code inspections to reduce errors in program development, *IBM Syst. J.*, 38, pp. 258–287.

104. Sommerville, I. (2011). *Software Engineering*, 9th Ed., Chapter 7 "Design and Implementation," (Addison Wesley, New York) pp. 176–204.

105. Sommerville, I. (2011). *Software Engineering*, 9th Ed., Chapter 8 "Software Testing," (Addison Wesley, New York) pp. 205–233.

106. Deitel, H. M., Deitel P. J., Nieto T. R. and McPhie D. C. (2001). *Perl: How to Program,* Chapter 3 "Control Structures: Part I," (Prentice Hall, Upper Saddle River) pp. 60–93.

107. Deitel, H. and Deitel, P. (2019). *Python for Programmers with Introductory AI Case Studies,* Chapter 1 "Introduction to Computers and Python," (Prentice Hall, New York) pp. 1–30.

108. Python [www.python.org]

109. R [www.r-project.org/about.html]

110. Octave [www.gnu.org/software/octave/about.html]

111. Anaconda [www.anaconda.com/distribution]

112. Jupyter [www.jupyter.org/install]

113. Quick Start for Numpy [www.numpy.org/devdocs/user/quickstart. html]

114. Severance, C. (2013). *Python for Informatics: Exploring Information*, Chapter 4 "Functions," (CreateSpace) pp. 43–56.

115. numpy.square [www.numpy.org/doc/stable/reference/generated/ numpy.square.html]

116. Numpy [www.numpy.org]

117. GitHub [www.github.com]

118. GitHub for Numpy [www.github.com/numpy]

119. Stackoverflow [www.stackoverflow.com]

120. Kaizen [www.us.kaizen.com]

121. Kaizen Glossary [www.kaizen.com/learn-kaizen/glossary.html]

122. Severance, C. (2013). *Python for Informatics: Exploring Information*, (CreateSpace).

123. LeMoyne, R., Kerr, W., Mastroianni, T. and Hessel, A. (2014). Implementation of machine learning for classifying hemiplegic gait disparity through use of a force plate, *Proc. 13th International Conference on Machine Learning and Applications (ICMLA), IEEE*, pp. 379–382.

124. LeMoyne, R., Mastroianni, T., Hessel, A. and Nishikawa, K. (2015). Implementation of machine learning for classifying prosthesis type through conventional gait analysis, *Proc. 37th Annual International Conference of the IEEE, Engineering in Medicine and Biology Society (EMBS)*, pp. 202–205.

125. LeMoyne, R., Mastroianni, T., Hessel, A. and Nishikawa, K. (2015). Application of a multilayer perceptron neural network for classifying software platforms of a powered prosthesis through a force plate, *Proc. 14th International Conference on Machine Learning and Applications (ICMLA), IEEE*, pp. 402–405.

126. LeMoyne, R. and Mastroianni, T. (2019). Classification of software control architectures for a powered prosthesis through conventional gait analysis using machine learning applications, *J. Mech. Med. Biol.*, 19, 1950044.

127. Deitel, H. and Deitel, P. (2019). *Python for Programmers with Introductory AI Case Studies*, Chapter 5 "Sequences: Lists and Tuples," (Prentice Hall, New York) pp. 101–136.

128. Python Library [docs.python.org/3/library]

129. Severance, C. (2013). *Python for Informatics: Exploring Information*, Chapter 5 "Iteration," (CreateSpace) pp. 57–66.

130. Severance, C. (2013). *Python for Informatics: Exploring Information*, Chapter 3 "Conditional Execution," (CreateSpace) pp. 31–42.

131. Severance, C. (2013). *Python for Informatics: Exploring Information*, Chapter 8 "Lists," (CreateSpace) pp. 91–106.

132. Severance, C. (2013). *Python for Informatics: Exploring Information*, Chapter 2 "Variables, Expressions and Statements," (CreateSpace) pp. 19–30.

133. McIlroy, M. D. (1968). Mass-Produced Software Components, *Proc. NATO Software Engineering Conference*, pp. 138–156.

134. Sommerville, I. (2011). *Software Engineering*, 9th Ed., Chapter 16 "Software Reuse," (Addison Wesley, New York) pp. 425–451.

135. Quinlan, J. R. (1993). *C4.5 Programs for Machine Learning*, Chapter 1 "Introduction," (Morgan Kaufmann Publishers, San Mateo) pp. 1–16.

136. Quinlan, J. R. (1993). *C4.5: Programs for Machine Learning*, (Morgan Kaufmann Publishers, San Mateo).

137. Quinlan, J. R. (1986). Induction of decision trees, *Mach. Learn.*, 1, pp. 81–106.

138. Wu, X., Kumar, V., Quinlan, J. R., Ghosh, J., Yang, Q., Motoda, H., McLachlan, G. J., Ng, A., Liu, B., Philip, S. Y. and Zhou, Z. H. (2008). Top 10 algorithms in data mining, *Knowl. Inf. Syst.*, 14, pp. 1–37.

139. Harrington, P. (2012). *Machine Learning in Action*, Chapter 3 "Splitting Datasets One Feature at a Time: Decision Trees," (Manning Publications, Shelter Island) pp. 37–60.

140. Witten, I. H., Frank, E. and Hall, M. A. (2011). *Data Mining: Practical Machine Learning Tools and Techniques*, 3rd Ed., Chapter 4 "Algorithms: The Basic Methods," (Morgan Kaufmann Publishers, Burlington) pp. 85–145.

141. Fix, E. and Hodges Jr., J. L. (1951). *Discriminatory Analysis; Nonparametric Discrimination: Consistency Properties* (USAF School of Aviation Medicine, Randolph Field). Project Number 21-49-004, Report Number 4.

142. Witten, I. H., Frank, E. and Hall, M. A. (2011). *Data Mining: Practical Machine Learning Tools and Techniques*, 3rd Ed., Chapter 3 "Output: Knowledge Representation," (Morgan Kaufmann Publishers, Burlington) pp. 61–83.

143. Witten, I. H., Frank, E. and Hall, M. A. (2011). *Data Mining: Practical Machine Learning Tools and Techniques*, 3rd Ed., Chapter 11 "The Explorer," (Morgan Kaufmann Publishers, Burlington) pp. 407–494.

144. Le Cessie, S. and Van Houwelingen, J. C. (1992). Ridge estimators in logistic regression, *J. R. Stat. Soc. Ser. C (Appl. Stat.)*, 41, pp. 191–201.

145. Bayes, T. (1763). LII. An essay towards solving a problem in the doctrine of chances. By the late Rev. Mr. Bayes, FRS communicated by Mr. Price, in a letter to John Canton, *AMFR S. Philos. Trans. R. Soc. Lond.*, 53, pp. 370–418.

146. John, G. H. and Langley, P. (1995). Estimating continuous distributions in Bayesian classifiers, *Proc. 11th Conference on Uncertainty in Artificial Intelligence*.

147. Begg, R. K., Palaniswami, M. and Owen, B. (2005). Support vector machines for automated gait classification, *IEEE Trans. Biomed. Eng.*, 52, pp. 828–838.

148. Begg, R. and Kamruzzaman, J. (2005). A machine learning approach for automated recognition of movement patterns using basic, kinetic and kinematic gait data, *J. Biomech.*, 38, pp. 401–408.

149. Cortes, C. and Vapnik, V. (1995). Support vector networks, *Mach. Learn.*, 20, pp. 273–297.

150. Vapnik, V. N. (1999). *The Nature of Statistical Learning Theory*, 2nd Ed. (Springer-Verlag, New York).

151. Witten, I. H., Frank, E. and Hall, M. A. (2011). *Data Mining: Practical Machine Learning Tools and Techniques*, 3rd Ed., Chapter 6 "Implementations: Real Machine Learning Schemes," (Morgan Kaufmann Publishers, Burlington) pp. 191–304.

152. Platt, J. C. (1999). *Advances in Kernel Methods: Support Vector Learning*, eds. Schölkopf, B., Burges J. C. and Smola, A. J., Chapter 12 "Fast Training of Support Vector Machines Using Sequential Minimal Optimization," (The MIT Press Cambridge, Massachusetts) pp. 185–208.

153. Witten, I. H., Frank, E. and Hall, M. A. (2011). *Data Mining: Practical Machine Learning Tools and Techniques*, 3rd Ed., Chapter 8 "Ensemble Learning," (Morgan Kaufmann Publishers, Burlington) pp. 351–373.

154. Breiman, L. (2001). Random forests, *Mach. Learn.*, 45, pp. 5–32.

155. Kandel, E. R., Schwartz, J. H. and Jessell, T. M. (2000). *Principles of Neural Science*, 4th Ed., Chapter 2 "Nerve Cells and Behavior," (McGraw-Hill, New York) pp. 19–35.

156. Seeley, R. R., Stephens, T. D. and Tate, P. (2003). *Anatomy and Physiology*, 6th Ed., Chapter 11 "Function and Organization of Nervous Tissue," (McGraw-Hill, Boston) pp. 363–399.

157. Munakata, T. (2008). *Fundamentals of the New Artificial Intelligence: Neural, Evolutionary, Fuzzy and More*, 2nd Ed., Chapter 2 "Neural Networks: Fundamentals and the Backpropagation Model," (Springer, London) pp. 7–36.

158. Russell S. J. and Norvig P. (2010). *Artificial Intelligence: A Modern Approach*, 3rd Ed., Chapter 18 "Learning from Examples," (Prentice Hall, Upper Saddle River) pp. 693–767.

159. Bryson, A. E. and Ho Y. C. (1969). *Applied Optimal Control: Optimization, Estimation, and Control*, (Blaisdell Publishing, Waltham).

160. Russell S. J. and Norvig P. (2010). *Artificial Intelligence: A Modern Approach*, 3rd Ed., Chapter 1 "Introduction," (Prentice Hall, Upper Saddle River) pp. 1–33.

161. Witten, I. H., Frank, E. and Hall, M. A. (2011). *Data Mining: Practical Machine Learning Tools and Techniques*, 3rd Ed., Chapter 2 "Input: Concepts, Instances, and Attributes," (Morgan Kaufmann Publishers, Burlington) pp. 39–60.

162. Witten, I. H., Frank, E. and Hall, M. A. (2011). *Data Mining: Practical Machine Learning Tools and Techniques*, 3rd Ed., Chapter 5 "Credibility: Evaluating What's Been Learned," (Morgan Kaufmann Publishers, Burlington) pp. 147–187.

163. LeMoyne, R., Mastroianni, T., Whiting, D. and Tomycz, N. (2020). Parametric evaluation of deep brain stimulation parameter configurations for Parkinson's disease using a conformal wearable and wireless inertial sensor system and machine learning, *Proc. 42nd Annual International Conference of the IEEE, Engineering in Medicine and Biology Society (EMBS)*, pp. 3606–3611.

164. LeMoyne, R., Mastroianni, T., Whiting, D. and Tomycz, N. (2020). Distinction of an assortment of deep brain stimulation parameter configurations for treating Parkinson's disease using machine learning with quantification of tremor response through a conformal wearable and wireless inertial sensor, *Adv. Park. Dis.*, 9, pp. 21–39.

165. LeMoyne, R., Mastroianni, T., Whiting, D. and Tomycz, N. (2020). Application of deep learning to distinguish multiple deep brain stimulation parameter configurations for the treatment of Parkinson's disease, *Proc. 19th International Conference on Machine Learning and Applications (ICMLA), IEEE*, pp. 1106–1111.

166. LeMoyne, R., Mastroianni, T., Whiting, D. and Tomycz, N. (2021). Deep learning for differentiating parameter configurations of deep brain stimulation for treating Parkinson's disease incorporating conformal wearable and wireless inertial sensors as an evolution for Network Centric Therapy, *Proc. Society for Neuroscience Global Connectome: A Virtual Event*.

Chapter 2

General Concept of Preliminary Network Centric Therapy Applying Deep Brain Stimulation for Ameliorating Movement Disorders with Machine Learning Classification using Python Based on Feedback from a Smartphone as a Wearable and Wireless System

2.1 Introduction

In order to meaningfully apply a smartphone for the quantification of a movement disorder, such as essential tremor, as a wearable and wireless system with machine learning classification to distinguish between deep brain stimulation system set to 'On' and 'Off' status through the application of Python to provide automated post-processing of the recorded inertial sensor signal data, the fundamentals of movement disorder should be elucidated. The diagnosis and conventional treatment intervention are provided and contrasted for two well-known movement disorders: essential tremor and Parkinson's disease, which both involve disparate neuroanatomical origins for their symptoms [1–28]. The deep brain stimulation system constitutes a complex medical device and represents a promising means of treatment for both movement disorders, such as essential tremor and Parkinson's disease, with highly specialized targeting of the deep brain and numerous parameter configurations for resolving patient specific intervention [12, 29–38].

The application of an inertial sensor through a wearable and wireless system has been advocated for the uniquely objective quantified insight provided by the signal data for the acquisition of an optimal parameter configuration respective of deep brain stimulation [12, 37–62]. An issue is that in light of the numerous parameter configurations with modulation of amplitude, frequency, pulse width, and polarity the optimization process can be an inherently resource intensive endeavor [63–65]. Inertial sensor quantification constitutes a verifiable strategy for the clinician to determine the efficacy of the prescribed deep brain stimulation parameter configuration [39–62]. From a historical perspective ordinal scales have been a basis for quantified feedback, but they are inherently controversial in terms of reliability [66–69]. Wearable and wireless inertial sensor systems have been progressively introduced [70–76].

During 2010, LeMoyne *et al.* applied a smartphone as a wearable and wireless system for quantifying Parkinson's disease with the accelerometer signal conveyed as an email attachment through wireless connectivity to the Internet [43]. The quantification of the movement disorder conducted by LeMoyne *et al.* was enabled through the Vibration application available on the App Store for Apple by Diffraction Limited Design LLC [77]. The application is relevant to both the iPod (a portable media device) and the iPhone (a smartphone). Current evolutions of the application provide both the accelerometer and gyroscope signal data for recording, and segmented wireless inertial sensor node architectures have been implemented [43, 45–53, 55–62, 78–98].

The incorporation of machine learning enables the capability to distinguish between prescribed classes of a feature set [47–53, 55–62, 82, 85–99]. The machine learning classification is provided by the Waikato Environment for Knowledge Analysis (WEKA) through the consolidation of the inertial sensor signal data to an Attribute-Relation File Format (ARFF), which implies the utility of automation software for the post-processing [47–53, 55–62, 85–102]. The objective throughout the book emphasizes the role of machine learning classification to distinguish deep brain stimulation set to 'On' and 'Off' status for a subject with essential tremor conducting a reach and grasp task using objectively quantified feedback derived from the accelerometer signal of a smartphone constituting a wearable and wireless system with post-processing software automation enabled through Python.

2.2 Movement Disorders, such as Essential Tremor and Parkinson's Disease, a General Perspective and Treatment

Two highly prevalent movement disorders are essential tremor and Parkinson's disease [1–6]. Their incidences are both proportional to age with considerable impact to quality of life [2, 5, 6]. Essential tremor is more predominant with an occurrence roughly an order of magnitude greater than Parkinson's disease [4, 5]. Both movement disorders are conventionally treated through the application of medication and surgery [2, 4, 7–10]. Recently, the application of deep brain stimulation has been successfully applied as a therapeutic intervention [11, 12].

The movement disorder typically manifested by Parkinson's disease is characterized by resting tremor. In general, a subject with Parkinson's disease attenuates tremor when conducting a movement task [4, 13]. By contrast, essential tremor is frequently characterized by a kinetic tremor. Kinetic tremor displays movement disorder upon conducting a movement task, such as reaching and grasping an object [2]. Through expert clinical observation essential tremor and Parkinson's disease can be readily diagnosed [14–21].

Beyond the disparity between resting and kinetic tremor, the actual frequency range of the tremor movement disorder is notably discernible [2, 4, 13]. The tremor derived from Parkinson's disease is standardly bound within the range of 4 to 5 Hertz [4, 13]. By comparison, essential tremor is represented by a great bandwidth at a higher frequency. Tremor associated with essential tremor is typically bound between 4 and 12 Hertz [2]. With a means to record and measure the actual tremor characteristics, essential tremor and Parkinson's disease can be readily diagnosed, and inertial sensors have been successfully demonstrated for the quantified differentiation between these two forms of movement disorder [22].

In conjunction with the clinically discernible disparity between essential tremor and Parkinson's disease, their neuroanatomical origins are relatively disparate [2, 4, 7, 8, 21, 23, 24]. Parkinson's disease involves the progressive degeneration of the dopaminergic neurons situated in the substantia nigra. This degenerative proclivity leads to dysfunction of the basal ganglia [4, 21, 23]. However, the neurological origins of essential tremor are less established. Dysfunction about the cerebellum and associated cerebello-thalamo-cortical pathway have been a central theme to proposed neurological mechanisms causing essential tremor [2, 7, 8, 24]. Intuitively, the lack of a distinctly determined neurological mechanism, challenges the ability to provide a standardized medical intervention [2, 7].

Traditionally, preliminary intervention for the treatment of a neurologically degenerative movement disorder, such as essential tremor and Parkinson's disease, involves the administration of particular medication [4, 8, 10]. For Parkinson's disease, levodopa is prescribed to attenuate movement disorder symptoms [4, 8, 21, 25]. Propranolol is standard for treating essential tremor, and it is also pertinent toward the medical therapy for Parkinson's disease [2, 7, 8, 21].

An assortment of alternative medical strategies is available for the treatment of essential tremor and Parkinson's disease. In the event that medical therapy becomes intractable, a conventional intervention of last resort involves permanent disruption of deep brain structure neurological pathways. An example is the thalamotomy, which involves dislocating neurological pathways associated with the thalamus achieved through thermal coagulation [2, 4, 10, 26–28]. Naturally, this neurosurgical technique infers permanent consequences.

By contrast, a novel neurosurgical technique that can be uniquely parameterized to accommodate a subject with a progressive neurodegenerative movement disorder, such as Parkinson's disease or essential tremor, is known as deep brain stimulation [29–31]. Furthermore, if this therapy strategy is deemed inefficacious, the deep brain stimulation apparatus can be removed with an essentially minimal impact to the patient [32]. Deep brain stimulation offers a preferable alternative to the permanency of the disruption of deep brain structure neurological pathways, such as through the thalamotomy [21, 33].

During 1987, Dr. Benabid and his colleagues demonstrated the efficacy of treating movement disorder, such as Parkinson's disease [30, 31]. Currently, both essential tremor and Parkinson's disease symptoms can be ameliorated though the application of deep brain stimulation that targets the ventral intermediate nucleus (VIM), which is associated with the motor aspects of the thalamus while receiving cerebellar input [30–32, 34]. Stereotactic neurosurgery is an inherent aspect of implanting a deep brain stimulation system [35]. The deep brain stimulation system is a complex medical device that consists of multiple components and subsystems [33]. These complexities warrant further discussion.

2.3 Deep Brain Stimulation for the Treatment of Movement Disorders, such as Essential Tremor and Parkinson's Disease

The deep brain stimulation system constitutes a complex medical device that is comprised of multiple primary subsystems and components. The electric signal generated by the deep brain stimulation system that attenuates movement disorder originates from the implantable pulse generator, which is illustrated in Figure 2.1. The energy source for the implantable pulse generator is derived from a battery. However, the significance of the battery is revealed in consideration of the observation that it is implanted in the patient. This consideration underscores the importance of acquiring a configuration parameter that properly conserves energy [12, 33, 35].

Emanating from the implantable pulse generator is the wire that extends to the targeted structure of the deep brain. At the end of the wire is the electrode that deposits a predetermined quantity of electrical energy upon the targeted structure of the deep brain, such as the VIM of the thalamus. Figure 2.2 presents an illustration of the wire and electrode associated with the implantable pulse generator [12, 33].

As implicated by the characteristics of the deep brain stimulation system, the implantation surgery to install the device is quite sophisticated. Precise stereotactic apparatus, as included in Figure 2.3, is applied for the implantation of the electrode and associated wire to

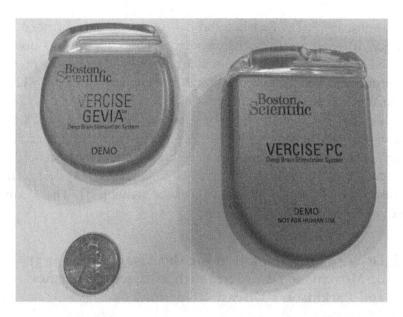

Fig. 2.1. The implantable pulse generator of the deep brain stimulation system provided by Allegheny General Hospital.

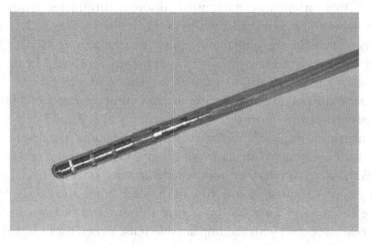

Fig. 2.2. Electrode and wire for the implantable pulse generator of the deep brain stimulation system provided by Allegheny General Hospital.

Fig. 2.3. Stereotactic apparatus for implanting deep brain stimulation electrodes provided by Allegheny General Hospital.

target the deep brain anatomical structure. The second aspect of the surgical procedure primarily consists of the installation of the implantable pulse generator. Intuitively, the surgical procedure to implant the deep brain stimulation apparatus is critical for the therapeutic efficacy [35, 36]. Likewise, the acquisition of an optimal parameter configuration regarding the deep brain stimulation system is instrumental for a patient specific intervention [12, 37, 38].

The clinical acquisition of an optimal parameter configuration for the efficacious administration of deep brain stimulation to ameliorate movement disorder symptoms, such as with respect to essential tremor and Parkinson's disease, is imperative for therapeutic efficacy, which has been advocated through the application of an inertial sensor [12, 37–62]. The clinician is presented with numerous permutations to achieve the optimal parameter configuration, which infers the inherently resource intensive nature of the endeavor [63]. The deep brain stimulation system is comprised of four distinct parameters:

- Amplitude
- Frequency
- Pulse width
- Polarity [12]

The polarity defines the current distribution proximal to the targeted structure of the deep brain [12, 64]. Temporal aspects of the stimulation current are regulated by the parameters representing frequency, also known as rate of stimulation, and pulse width. The stimulation frequency is based on the quantity of stimulating pulses per second defined by Hertz. The pulse width, which is represented by microseconds, is the duration of the stimulating pulse. The stimulating amplitude based on current source is represented by milliamperes, and for the voltage source technique volts [12].

With the considerable assortment of parameter configurations available, the clinician may also establish an interleaved parameter configuration. The interleaved parameter configuration involves assigning a series of multiple sequential parameter configurations to the deep brain stimulation system. This feature of the device further enables patient specific therapeutic intervention [12].

The acquisition of a relatively optimal parameter configuration presents a time intensive endeavor for the clinician that is iterative in nature and can last for approximately weeks to months [63]. The clinical programmer for assigning the parameter configuration for the deep brain stimulation system is presented in Figure 2.4. The patient is equipped with the patient programmer represented in Figure 2.5. Researchers have even proposed the allocation of specialized multidisciplinary teams for programing the deep brain stimulation system parameter configuration [65]. Quantified feedback presents a means for clinicians to verify the efficacy of the deep brain stimulation parameter configuration [39–62].

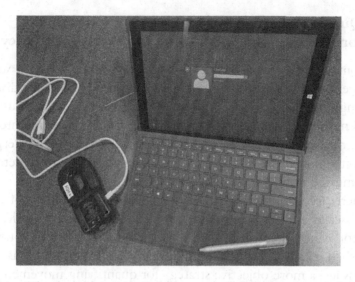

Fig. 2.4. The deep brain stimulation system clinical programmer for acquisition of a parameter configuration at the discretion of the clinician provided by Allegheny General Hospital.

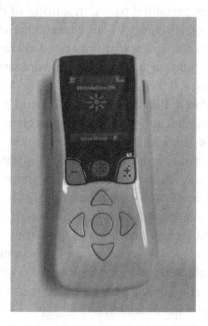

Fig. 2.5. The deep brain stimulation system patient programmer provided by Allegheny General Hospital.

2.4 Quantification of Movement Disorder Status for Ascertaining Therapeutic Intervention Efficacy

The conventional means of quantifying the status of a person with a movement disorder, such as essential tremor and Parkinson's disease, is through the ordinal scale. An ordinal scale spans a specific range of ranked numbers, such as zero to four. Each ranking is represented by a series of qualitative criteria, for which an expert clinician interprets a subject's movement disorder and applies a subjective interpretation regarding the ordinal scale [14–20].

There are multiple issues for this approach. Reliability of these ordinal scales is a subject of contention [66–69]. Multiple scales also exist, for which there is furthermore the issue that there is not an established means to translate findings between scales [14]. Based on these issues, a more objective strategy for quantifying movement disorder would be highly desirable, such as the application of wearable and wireless inertial sensor systems [39–62].

Preliminary introduction of accelerometer systems for quantifying movement disorders pertained to the mounting of them as functionally wearable devices. Preliminary accelerometers demonstrated the capacity to establish the efficacy of prescribed therapy [70–75]. This nascent capability would further evolve to the domain of wearable and wireless inertial sensor systems [39–62].

Through simulated Parkinson's disease hand tremor, LeMoyne *et al.* demonstrated the utility of wireless accelerometers that were effectively wearable through securing the wireless accelerometer to the dorsum of the hand through a glove, as illustrated in Figure 2.6. The wireless pathway involved connectivity between the wireless accelerometer and local laptop computer [40–42, 44, 45]. Figures 2.7 and 2.8 demonstrate the acceleration waveforms for both the static and simulated tremor scenarios [44]. Within this evolutionary timeframe another device for quantifying movement disorder related hand tremor was achieved through the Kinesia™, which incorporated a ring mounted inertial sensor with a wire connecting to a command module for wireless transmission [76].

Fig. 2.6. Apparatus for wireless accelerometer system for quantifying hand tremor [44].

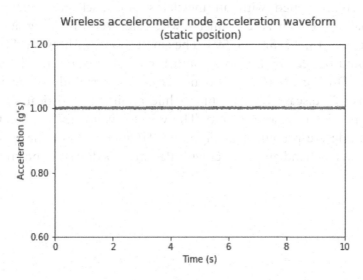

Fig. 2.7. Wireless accelerometer system with static condition [44].

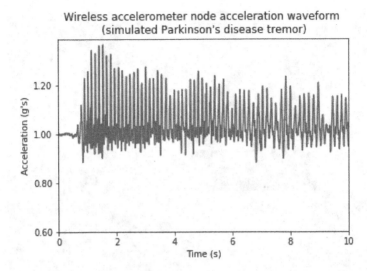

Fig. 2.8.   Wireless accelerometer system with simulated Parkinson's disease tremor [44].

The next evolution of wearable and wireless inertial sensor systems incorporated the capabilities of the smartphone. The smartphone is equipped with an inertial sensor package, which was originally solely an accelerometer with later versions integrating a gyroscope [43, 45–53, 55–59]. The smartphone as shown in Figure 2.9 could be readily mounted about the dorsum of the hand with a glove. During 2010, LeMoyne *et al.* successfully quantified Parkinson's disease hand tremor while attaining statistical significance relative to a steady hand. The waveforms for the acceleration magnitude are presented in Figures 2.10 and 2.11 for the subject with a steady hand and subject with Parkinson's disease hand tremor [43].

Fig. 2.9.   Smartphone mounted about the dorsum of the hand for quantifying hand tremor, such as for Parkinson's disease [43].

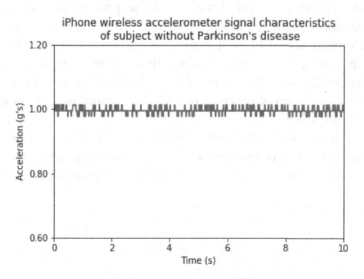

Fig. 2.10.   Smartphone accelerometer signal for a steady hand [43].

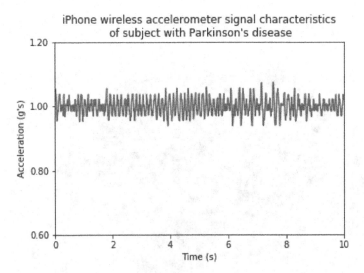

Fig. 2.11.   Smartphone accelerometer signal for Parkinson's disease hand tremor [43].

Another significant finding of the research by LeMoyne *et al.* was the observation that the experiment was conducted in metropolitan Pittsburgh, Pennsylvania, and the post-processing of the data occurred in the greater region of Los Angeles, California. The accelerometer signal of each experimental trial was wirelessly conveyed by connectivity to the Internet through an email attachment. In essence, the Internet access to the respective email account constituted a functional semblance of a Cloud computing environment [43, 45–53, 55–59].

As an extension to the utilities of the smartphone for quantifying progressively neurodegenerative movement disorders, such as Parkinson's disease and essential tremor, LeMoyne *et al.* during 2015 successfully ascertained the efficacy of deep brain stimulation respective of 'On' and 'Off' status for the treatment of essential tremor through a smartphone functioning as a wearable and wireless accelerometer platform through machine learning classification. Further studies were later applied to acquiring inertial sensor feature sets represented by both the accelerometer and gyroscope. These endeavors successfully differentiated deep brain stimulation 'On' and 'Off' status for both Parkinson's disease and essential tremor using an assortment of machine learning classification algorithms [47–53, 55–59].

2.5 Smartphone Wearable and Wireless Inertial Sensor System

For the movement disorder quantification studies and associated research conducted by LeMoyne *et al.*, the Vibration application available on the App Store for Apple by Diffraction Limited Design LLC has been selected [77]. The application is amendable for operation on both the iPod (a portable media device) and the iPhone (a smartphone). Since the preliminary use of the Vibration application by LeMoyne *et al.* during 2010, it has considerably evolved. For example, the current version of the application supports recording for both the accelerometer and gyroscope signal data [43, 45–53, 55–59, 78–87, 89–98].

The application emails each respective experimental trial as a Microsoft Excel Comma-Separated Values (CSV) file attachment, which is readily available for post-processing. Figure 2.12 illustrates a sample of the accelerometer signal data recorded by the Vibration application. The **Settings** panel regulates the **Data Source** and

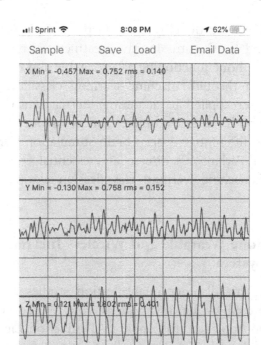

Fig. 2.12.   Vibration application for the smartphone with a graph of the accelerometer data [77].

Data Acquisition Settings as displayed in Figure 2.13. The associated **Data Source** panel determines the selected inertial sensor signal, such as the accelerometer or the gyroscope, as revealed in

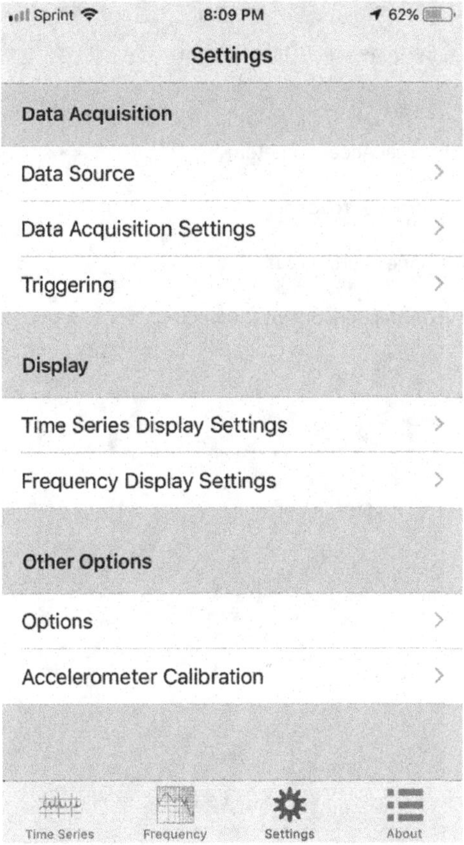

Fig. 2.13.   Vibration application for the smartphone, **Settings** panel [77].

Figure 2.14. The **Data Acquisition Settings** panel consists of multiple parameters, such as sampling rate (1–100 Hz), sample delay (0–60 seconds), and sample length (spanning between

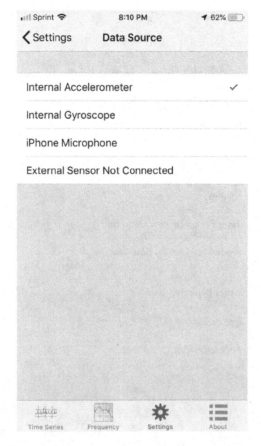

Fig. 2.14. Vibration application for the smartphone, **Data Source** panel [77].

approximately 5 and 82 seconds), which as presented in Figure 2.15 [43, 45–53, 55–59, 78–87, 89–98].

The operation of the smartphone representing a wearable and wireless inertial sensor system constitutes a preliminary version of Network Centric Therapy. The intrinsic inertial

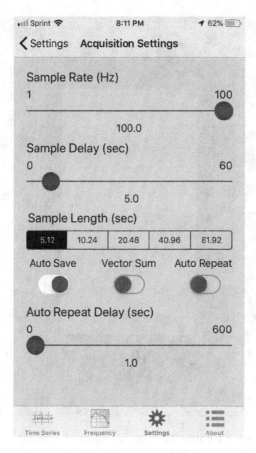

Fig. 2.15. Vibration application for the smartphone, **Data Acquisition Settings** panel [77].

sensor package of the smartphone can quantify human movement at the convenience of the subject's preference with the signal data conveyed wirelessly through connectivity to the Internet as an email package for post-processing anywhere in

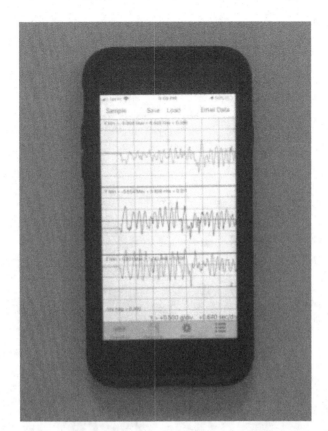

Fig. 2.16.   Network Centric Therapy represented through a smartphone as a wearable and wireless inertial sensor system.

the world. The email resource constitutes a functional version of a Cloud computing environment [43, 45–53, 55–59, 78–87, 89–98]. Figure 2.16 presents a smartphone representative for Network Centric Therapy.

2.6 Machine Learning and Software Automation

Machine learning augments the post-processing capability of Network Centric Therapy with the ability to differentiate between two disparate classes of a feature set [47–53, 55–62, 82, 86–99]. The ability to distinguish between a deep brain stimulation system set to 'On' and 'Off'

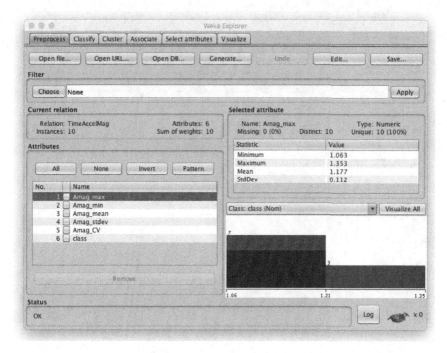

Fig. 2.17. The Weka Explorer **Preprocess** panel [47, 100–102].

status for subjects with essential tremor and Parkinson's disease has been achieved through the application of WEKA. Each experimental trial consisting of inertial sensor signal data is represented as an instance. Respective of each instance a series of numeric attributes characterizing the inertial sensor signal data are assigned to assemble the feature set. The feature set is assembled into an ARFF file, such as through automation software [47–53, 55–62, 83, 86–102]. Figures 2.17 and 2.18 represent the Weka Explorer **Preprocess** and **Classify** panels.

In principle, the inertial sensor data represented as a CSV file derived from the Vibration application for the smartphone (iPhone) can be manually assembled to develop an ARFF file [47–53, 55–59, 62, 82, 86, 87, 89–100]. However, the establishment of automation software can greatly facilitate the consolidation of the inertial sensor signal data into an ARFF file for machine learning classification through WEKA [47–53, 55–62, 83, 86–102]. A highly desirable

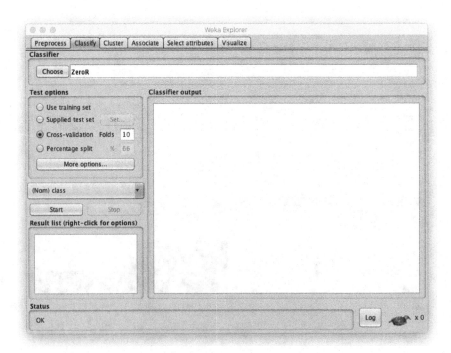

Fig. 2.18.   The Weka Explorer **Classify** panel [47, 100–102].

programming language for achieving this goal is Python. In order to successfully implement Python to automate the consolidation of the inertial sensor signal data into an ARFF file, a representation of the software development process involving a thorough and strategic phase prior to actual software programming, such as the establishment of requirements and their comprehensive review, is discussed. Upon the development of preliminary software programming continuous improvement shall be implemented. These initial concepts for software engineering and development shall be detailed in the pending Chapter 3 'Global Algorithm Development'.

2.7 The Objective of Machine Learning Classification for 'On' and 'Off' Status of Deep Brain Stimulation for the Treatment of Essential Tremor with Python Applied to Automate the Consolidation of the ARFF File

As the prevalence of essential tremor is on the order of 10 times greater than Parkinson's disease, the scope of the objective shall emphasize a subject with essential tremor. The objective throughout the book shall focus on machine learning classification to differentiate between deep brain stimulation set to 'On' and 'Off' status for a subject with essential tremor performing a reach and grasp task incorporating objectively quantified feedback derived from the accelerometer signal of a smartphone representing a wearable and wireless system with post-processing software automation achieved through Python. This demonstration from the perspective of engineering proof of concept presents the preliminary capability of Network Centric Therapy for the treatment of progressively degenerative movement disorders. The data is derived from the IEEE EMBC 2015 conference publication 'Implementation of a smartphone wireless accelerometer platform for establishing deep brain stimulation treatment efficacy of essential tremor with machine learning' by Robert LeMoyne (Ph.D.), Nestor Tomycz (M.D.), Timothy Mastroianni, Cyrus McCandless (Ph.D.), Michael Cozza, and David Peduto (Lt. Col. Ret.) [47].

The efficacy of the deep brain stimulation system respective of 'On' and 'Off' status shall be differentiated through conducting a reach and grasp task involving a flexible bandage placed on a table as illustrated in Figure 2.19. The smartphone shall be mounted to the dorsum of the hand through a latex glove. With the smartphone activated to record the acceleration signal the subject shall then reach and grasp the flexible bandage. The smartphone shall then convey the signal by wireless connectivity as an email attachment for post-processing [47]. Using Python to post-process the trial data, an ARFF file shall be developed for machine learning classification using WEKA. Subsequently, the classification accuracy and performance of

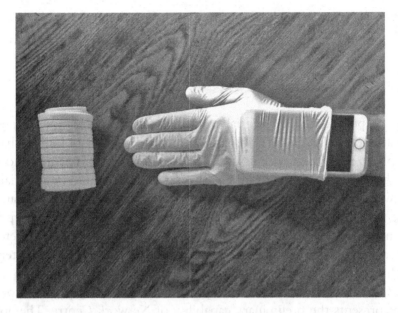

Fig. 2.19.   Smartphone as a wearable and wireless system mounted with latex glove and flexible bandage for conducting the reach and grasp task [47].

seven machine learning algorithms available from WEKA shall be evaluated:

- J48 decision tree
- K-nearest neighbors
- Logistic regression
- Naïve Bayes
- Support vector machine
- Random forest
- Multilayer perceptron neural network

The advent of Network Centric Therapy for the treatment of neurodegenerative movement disorders, such as Parkinson's disease and essential tremor, through machine learning is anticipated to radically advance the quality and efficacy of therapeutic intervention. This capability is especially expected to advance the optimization process of converging upon deep brain stimulation parameter configurations with eventual closed-loop automated tuning [33, 53–57, 100–102]. Furthermore, Network Centric Therapy is envisioned to provide augmented situational awareness for clinicians with respect to attaining the optimal treatment strategy [53, 95, 103, 104].

2.8 Conclusion

The scope of the objective is to apply a smartphone as a wearable and wireless system for the quantification of essential tremor during a reach and grasp task. The quantified inertial sensor signal data provide an objectively quantified contrast with respect to a deep brain stimulation system set to 'On' and 'Off' status. Using machine learning enabled through WEKA classification accuracy is achieved to distinguish between the two disparate deep brain stimulation scenarios. Given the nature of the accelerometer signal data, a means of automated post-processing is recommended, which is provided by the application of Python for consolidating the signal data into a feature set.

Preliminarily, the foundation and conventional treatment for movement disorders are addressed, such as for essential tremor and also Parkinson's disease. The application of deep brain stimulation constitutes an advanced concept for the treatment of movement disorder symptoms. However, an associated issue is the inherently resource intensive nature for acquiring an optimal parameter configuration. A robust means of quantifying the nature of the response to various deep brain stimulation parameter configurations would be advantageous for the treatment of movement disorder symptoms.

Wearable and wireless inertial sensor systems have been progressively evolved to evaluate the status and intervention efficacy for movement disorders, such as essential tremor and Parkinson's disease. Equipped with a unique software application the smartphone has been applied for the quantification of movement disorder tremor symptoms. The smartphone can readily be mounted to the dorsum of the hand and represents a functionally wearable and wireless inertial sensor system.

Software automation, such as through Python, post-processes the inertial sensor signal data to a feature set conforming to the ARFF file imperative for conducting machine learning through WEKA. In order to develop a Python software automation program to satisfy the objective of the book, an incremental and organized process is applied. Chapter 3 'Global Algorithm Development' emphasizes the significance of developing requirements and pseudo code with the subsequent selection of Python implemented through the Jupyter Notebook.

References

1. Parkinson, J. (1817). *An Essay on the Shaking Palsy*, (Whittingham and Rowland, London).
2. Louis, E. D. (2005). Essential tremor, *Lancet Neurol.*, 4, pp. 100–110.
3. Louis, E. D. (2000). Essential tremor, *Arch. Neurol. (JAMA Neurol.)*, 57, pp. 1522–1524.
4. Kandel, E. R., Schwartz, J. H. and Jessell, T. M. (2000). *Principles of Neural Science*, 4th Ed., Chapter 43 "The Basal Ganglia," (McGraw-Hill, New York) pp. 853–867.
5. Essential Tremor [www.essentialtremor.org]
6. Seeley, R. R., Stephens, T. D. and Tate, P. (2003). *Anatomy and Physiology*, 6th Ed., Chapter 14 "Integration of Nervous System Functions," (McGraw-Hill, Boston,) pp. 465–500.
7. Deuschl, G., Raethjen, J., Hellriegel, H. and Elble, R. (2011). Treatment of patients with essential tremor, *Lancet Neurol.*, 10, pp. 148–161.
8. Habib-ur-Rehman. (2000). Diagnosis and management of tremor, *Arch. Intern. Med.*, 160, pp. 2438–2444.
9. LeMoyne, R., Mastroianni, T., Whiting, D. and Tomycz, N. (2019). *Wearable and Wireless Systems for Healthcare II: Movement Disorder Evaluation and Deep Brain Stimulation Systems*, Chapter 1 "Wearable and Wireless Systems for Movement Disorder Evaluation and Deep Brain Stimulation Systems," (Springer, Singapore) pp. 1–15.

10. Nolte, J. and Sundsten, J. W. (2002). *The Human Brain: An Introduction to its Functional Anatomy*, 5th Ed., Chapter 19 "Basal Ganglia," (Mosby, St. Louis) pp. 464–485.

11. Williams, R. (2010). Alim-Louis Benabid: Stimulation and serendipity, *Lancet Neurol.*, 9, p. 1152.

12. Amon, A. and Alesch, F. (2017). Systems for deep brain stimulation: Review of technical features, *J. Neural. Transm.*, 124, pp. 1083–1091.

13. Bickley, L. S. and Szilagyi, P. G. (2003). *Bates' Guide to Physical Examination and History Taking*, 8th Ed., Chapter 17 "The Nervous System," (Lippincott Williams and Wilkins, Philadelphia) pp. 681–764.

14. Ramaker, C., Marinus, J., Stiggelbout, A. M. and Van Hilten, B. J. (2002). Systematic evaluation of rating scales for impairment and disability in Parkinson's disease, *Mov. Disord.*, 17, pp. 867–876.

15. Fahn, S., Elton, R. and UPDRS Development Committee. (1987). *Recent Developments in Parkinson's Disease, Vol. 2.*, eds. Fahn, S., Marsden, C. D., Calne, D. B. and Goldstein, M., "Unified Parkinson's Disease Rating Scale," (Macmillan Health Care Information, Florham Park) pp. 153–163, 293–304.

16. Goetz, C. G., Stebbins, G. T., Chmura, T. A., Fahn, S., Poewe, W. and Tanner, C. M. (2010). Teaching program for the Movement Disorder Society-sponsored revision of the Unified Parkinson's Disease Rating Scale: (MDS-UPDRS), *Mov. Disord.*, 25, pp. 1190–1194.

17. Movement Disorder Society Task Force on Rating Scales for Parkinson's Disease. (2003). The Unified Parkinson's Disease Rating Scale (UPDRS): Status and recommendations, *Mov. Disord.*, 18, pp. 738–750.

18. Goetz, C. G., Tilley, B. C., Shaftman, S. R., Stebbins, G. T., Fahn, S., Martinez-Martin, P., Poewe, W., Sampaio, C., Stern, M. B., Dodel, R., Dubois, B., Holloway, R., Jankovic, J., Kulisevsky, J., Lang, A. E., Lees, A., Leurgans, S., LeWitt, P. A., Nyenhuis, D., Olanow, C. W., Rascol, O., Schrag, A., Teresi, J. A., van Hilten, J. J. and LaPelle, N. (2008). Movement Disorder Society-sponsored revision of the Unified Parkinson's Disease Rating Scale (MDS-UPDRS): Scale presentation and clinimetric testing results, *Mov. Disord.*, 23, pp. 2129–2170.

19. Fahn, S., Tolosa, E. and Marin, C. (1988). *Parkinson's Disease and Movement Disorders*, Chapter 17 "Clinical Rating Scale for Tremor," (Urban & Schwarzenberg, Baltimore) pp. 225–234.

20. Elble, R. J. (2016). The essential tremor rating assessment scale, *J. Neurol. Neuromed.*, 1, pp. 34–38.

21. LeMoyne, R., Mastroianni, T., Whiting, D. and Tomycz, N. (2019). *Wearable and Wireless Systems for Healthcare II: Movement Disorder Evaluation and Deep Brain Stimulation Systems*, Chapter 2 "Movement Disorders: Parkinson's Disease and Essential Tremor — A General Perspective," (Springer, Singapore) pp. 17–24.

22. Hossen, A., Muthuraman, M., Al-Hakim, Z., Raethjen, J., Deuschl, G. and Heute, U. (2013). Discrimination of Parkinsonian tremor from essential tremor using statistical signal characterization of the spectrum of accelerometer signal, *Biomed. Mater. Eng.*, 23, pp. 513–531.

23. Diamond, M. C., Scheibel, A. B. and Elson, L. M. (1985). *The Human Brain Coloring Book*, Chapter 5 "Introduction: The Brain," (Harper Perennial, New York) pp. 5–24, 5–25.

24. Paris-Robidas, S., Brochu, E., Sintes, M., Emond, V., Bousquet, M., Vandal, M., Pilote, M., Tremblay, C., Di Paolo, T., Rajput, A. H., Rajput, A. and Calon, F. (2012). Defective dentate nucleus GABA receptors in essential tremor, *Brain*, 135, pp. 105–116.

25. The Parkinson Study Group. (2004). Levodopa and the progression of Parkinson's disease, *N. Engl. J. Med.*, 351, pp. 2498–2508.

26. Giller, C. A., Dewey, R. B., Ginsburg, M. I., Mendelsohn, D. B. and Berk, A. M. (1998). Stereotactic pallidotomy and thalamotomy using individual variations of anatomic landmarks for localization, *Neurosurgery*, 42, pp. 56–65.

27. Niranjan, A., Kondziolka, D., Baser, S., Heyman, R. and Lunsford, L. D. (2000). Functional outcomes after gamma knife thalamotomy for essential tremor and MS-related tremor, *Neurology*, 55, pp. 443–446.

28. Young, R. F., Jacques, S., Mark, R., Kopyov, O., Copcutt, B., Posewitz, A. and Li, F. (2000). Gamma knife thalamotomy for treatment of tremor: Long-term results, *J. Neurosurg.*, 93, pp. 128–135.

29. Flora, E. D., Perera, C. L., Cameron, A. L. and Maddern, G. J. (2010). Deep brain stimulation for essential tremor: A systematic review, *Mov. Disord.*, 25, pp. 1550–1559.

30. Miocinovic, S., Somayajula, S., Chitnis, S. and Vitek, J. L. (2013). History, applications, and mechanisms of deep brain stimulation, *JAMA Neurol.*, 70, pp. 163–171.

31. Benabid, A. L., Pollak, P., Louveau, A., Henry, S. and de Rougemont, J. (1987). Combined (thalamotomy and stimulation) stereotactic surgery of the VIM thalamic nucleus for bilateral Parkinson's disease, *Appl. Neurophysiol.*, 50, pp. 344–346.

32. Yu, H. and Neimat, J. S. (2008). The treatment of movement disorders by deep brain stimulation, *Neurotherapeutics*, 5, pp. 26–36.

33. LeMoyne, R., Mastroianni, T., Whiting, D. and Tomycz, N. (2019). *Wearable and Wireless Systems for Healthcare II: Movement Disorder Evaluation and Deep Brain Stimulation Systems*, Chapter 4 "Deep Brain Stimulation for the Treatment of Movement Disorder Regarding Parkinson's Disease and Essential Tremor with Device Characterization," (Springer, Singapore) pp. 37–51.

34. Hassler, R. (1959). Introduction to Stereotaxis with an Atlas of the Human Brain, eds. Schaltenbrand G. and Bailey P. "Anatomy of the Thalamus," (Thieme, Stuttgart) pp. 230–290.

35. LeMoyne, R., Mastroianni, T., Whiting, D. and Tomycz, N. (2019). *Wearable and Wireless Systems for Healthcare II: Movement Disorder Evaluation and Deep Brain Stimulation Systems*, Chapter 5 "Surgical Procedure for Deep Brain Stimulation Implantation and Operative Phase with Postoperative Risks," (Springer, Singapore) pp. 53–63.

36. Constantoyannis, C., Berk, C., Honey, C. R., Mendez, I. and Brownstone, R. M. (2005). Reducing hardware-related complications of deep brain stimulation, *Can. J. Neurol. Sci.*, 32, pp. 194–200.

37. Volkmann, J., Moro, E. and Pahwa, R. (2006). Basic algorithms for the programming of deep brain stimulation in Parkinson's disease, *Mov. Disord.*, 21, pp. S284–S289.

38. Isaias, I. U. and Tagliati, M. (2008). *Deep Brain Stimulation in Neurological and Psychiatric Disorders*, eds. Tarsy, D., Vitek, J. L., Starr, P. A. and Okun, M. S., Chapter 20 "Deep Brain Stimulation Programming for Movement Disorders," (Springer, New York) pp. 361–397.

39. LeMoyne, R. (2007). Gradient optimized neuromodulation for Parkinson's disease, *Proc. 12th Annual UCLA Research Conference on Aging*.

40. LeMoyne, R., Coroian, C. and Mastroianni, T. (2008). 3D wireless accelerometer characterization of Parkinson's disease status, *Proc. Plasticity and Repair in Neurodegenerative Disorders*.

41. LeMoyne, R., Coroian, C., Mastroianni, T., Opalinski, P., Cozza, M. and Grundfest, W. (2009). *Biomedical Engineering*, ed. Barros de Mello, C. A., Chapter 10 "The Merits of Artificial Proprioception, with Applications in Biofeedback Gait Rehabilitation Concepts and Movement Disorder Characterization," (InTech, Vienna) pp. 165–198.

42. LeMoyne, R., Coroian, C. and Mastroianni, T. (2009). Quantification of Parkinson's disease characteristics using wireless accelerometers, *Proc. ICME International Conference on IEEE Complex Medical Engineering (CME)*, pp. 1–5.

43. LeMoyne, R., Mastroianni, T., Cozza, M., Coroian, C. and Grundfest, W. (2010). Implementation of an iPhone for characterizing Parkinson's disease tremor through a wireless accelerometer application, *Proc. 32nd Annual International Conference of the IEEE, Engineering in Medicine and Biology Society (EMBS)*, pp. 4954–4958.

44. LeMoyne, R., Mastroianni, T. and Grundfest, W. (2013). Wireless accelerometer configuration for monitoring Parkinson's disease hand tremor, *Adv. Park. Dis.*, 2, pp. 62–67.

45. LeMoyne, R. (2013). Wearable and wireless accelerometer systems for monitoring Parkinson's disease patients — a perspective review, *Adv. Park. Dis.*, 2, pp. 113–115.

46. LeMoyne, R. and Mastroianni, T. (2015). *Mobile Health Technologies, Methods and Protocols*, eds. Rasooly, A. and Herold, K. E., Chapter 23 "Use of Smartphones and Portable Media Devices for Quantifying Human Movement Characteristics of Gait, Tendon Reflex Response, and Parkinson's Disease Hand Tremor," (Springer, New York) pp. 335–358.

47. LeMoyne, R., Tomycz, N., Mastroianni, T., McCandless, C., Cozza, M. and Peduto, D. (2015). Implementation of a smartphone wireless accelerometer platform for establishing deep brain stimulation treat-

ment efficacy of essential tremor with machine learning, *Proc. 37th Annual International Conference of the IEEE, Engineering in Medicine and Biology Society, (EMBS)*, pp. 6772–6775.

48. LeMoyne, R. and Mastroianni, T. (2016). *Telemedicine*, "Telemedicine Perspectives for Wearable and Wireless Applications Serving the Domain of Neurorehabilitation and Movement Disorder Treatment," (SMGroup, Dover, Delaware) pp. 1–10.

49. LeMoyne, R. and Mastroianni, T. (2017). *Smartphones from an Applied Research Perspective*, ed. Mohamudally, N., Chapter 1 "Smartphone and Portable Media Device: A Novel Pathway Toward the Diagnostic Characterization of Human Movement," (InTech, Rijeka, Croatia) pp. 1–24.

50. LeMoyne, R., Mastroianni, T., Tomycz, N., Whiting, D., Oh, M., McCandless, C., Currivan, C. and Peduto, D. (2017). Implementation of a multilayer perceptron neural network for classifying deep brain stimulation in 'On' and 'Off' modes through a smartphone representing a wearable and wireless sensor application, *Proc. 47th Society for Neuroscience Annual Meeting, Featured in Hot Topics (Top 1% of Abstracts)*.

51. LeMoyne, R., Mastroianni, T., McCandless, C., Currivan, C., Whiting, D. and Tomycz, N. (2018). Implementation of a smartphone as a wearable and wireless accelerometer and gyroscope platform for ascertaining deep brain stimulation treatment efficacy of Parkinson's disease through machine learning classification, *Adv. Park. Dis.*, 7, pp. 19–30.

52. LeMoyne, R., Mastroianni, T., McCandless, C., Currivan, C., Whiting, D. and Tomycz, N. (2018). Implementation of a smartphone as a wearable and wireless inertial sensor platform for determining efficacy of deep brain stimulation for Parkinson's disease tremor through machine learning, *Proc. 48th Society for Neuroscience Annual Meeting, Nanosymposium*.

53. LeMoyne, R., Mastroianni, T., Whiting, D. and Tomycz, N. (2019). *Wearable and Wireless Systems for Healthcare II: Movement Disorder Evaluation and Deep Brain Stimulation Systems*, (Springer, Singapore).

54. LeMoyne, R., Mastroianni, T., Whiting, D. and Tomycz, N. (2019). *Wearable and Wireless Systems for Healthcare II: Movement Disorder*

Evaluation and Deep Brain Stimulation Systems, Chapter 6 "Preliminary Wearable and Locally Wireless Systems for Quantification of Parkinson's Disease and Essential Tremor Characteristics," (Springer, Singapore) pp. 65–78.

55. LeMoyne, R., Mastroianni, T., Whiting, D. and Tomycz, N. (2019). *Wearable and Wireless Systems for Healthcare II: Movement Disorder Evaluation and Deep Brain Stimulation Systems,* Chapter 7 "Wearable and Wireless Systems with Internet Connectivity for Quantification of Parkinson's Disease and Essential Tremor Characteristics," (Springer, Singapore) pp. 79–97.

56. LeMoyne, R., Mastroianni, T., Whiting, D. and Tomycz, N. (2019). *Wearable and Wireless Systems for Healthcare II: Movement Disorder Evaluation and Deep Brain Stimulation Systems,* Chapter 8 "Role of Machine Learning for Classification of Movement Disorder and Deep Brain Stimulation Status," (Springer, Singapore) pp. 99–111.

57. LeMoyne, R., Mastroianni, T., Whiting, D. and Tomycz, N. (2019). *Wearable and Wireless Systems for Healthcare II: Movement Disorder Evaluation and Deep Brain Stimulation Systems,* Chapter 9 "Assessment of Machine Learning Classification Strategies for the Differentiation of Deep Brain Stimulation "On" and "Off" Status for Parkinson's Disease Using a Smartphone as a Wearable and Wireless Inertial Sensor for Quantified Feedback," (Springer, Singapore) pp. 113–126.

58. LeMoyne, R., Mastroianni, T., McCandless, C., Whiting, D. and Tomycz, N. (2019). Evaluation of machine learning algorithms for classifying deep brain stimulation respective of 'On' and 'Off' status, *Proc. 9th International IEEE Conference on Neural Engineering (NER), IEEE/EMBS,* pp. 483–488.

59. LeMoyne, R. and Mastroianni, T. (2019). *Smartphones: Recent Innovations and Applications,* ed. Dabove, P., Chapter 7 "Network Centric Therapy for Wearable and Wireless Systems," (Nova Science Publishers, Hauppauge).

60. LeMoyne, R., Mastroianni, T., Whiting, D. and Tomycz, N. (2019). Network Centric Therapy for deep brain stimulation status parametric analysis with machine learning classification, *Proc. 49th Society for Neuroscience Annual Meeting, Nanosymposium.*

61. LeMoyne, R., Mastroianni, T., Whiting, D. and Tomycz, N. (2019). Preliminary Network Centric Therapy for machine learning classification of deep brain stimulation status for the treatment of Parkinson's disease with a conformal wearable and wireless inertial sensor, *Adv. Park. Dis.*, 8, pp. 75–91.

62. LeMoyne, R. and Mastroianni, T. (2020). *Multilayer Perceptrons: Theory and Applications*, ed. Vang-Mata, R., Chapter 2, "Machine Learning Classification for Network Centric Therapy Utilizing the Multilayer Perceptron Neural Network," (Nova Science Publishers, Hauppauge) pp. 39–76.

63. Pretto, T. (2007). Deep brain stimulation, *Neurologist*, 13, pp. 103–104.

64. Butson, C. R. and McIntyre, C. C. (2008). Current steering to control the volume of tissue activated during deep brain stimulation, *Brain Stimul.*, 1, pp. 7–15.

65. Panisset, M., Picillo, M., Jodoin, N., Poon, Y. Y., Valencia-Mizrachi, A., Fasano, A., Munhoz, R. and Honey, C. R. (2017). Establishing a standard of care for deep brain stimulation centers in Canada, *Can. J. Neurol. Sci.*, 44, pp. 132–138.

66. Siderowf, A., McDermott, M., Kieburtz, K., Blindauer, K., Plumb, S. and Shoulson, I. (2002). Test-retest reliability of the unified Parkinson's disease rating scale in patients with early Parkinson's disease: Results from a multicenter clinical trial, *Mov. Disord.*, 17, pp. 758–763.

67. Metman, L. V., Myre, B., Verwey, N., Hassin-Baer, S., Arzbaecher, J., Sierens, D. and Bakay, R. (2004). Test-retest reliability of UPDRS-III, dyskinesia scales, and timed motor tests in patients with advanced Parkinson's disease: An argument against multiple baseline assessments, *Mov. Disord.*, 19, pp. 1079–1084.

68. Richards, M., Marder, K., Cote, L. and Mayeux, R. (1994). Interrater reliability of the Unified Parkinson's Disease Rating Scale motor examination, *Mov. Disord.*, 9, pp. 89–91.

69. Post, B., Merkus, M. P., de Bie, R. M., de Haan, R. J. and Speelman, J. D. (2005). Unified Parkinson's Disease Rating Scale motor examination: Are ratings of nurses, residents in neurology, and movement disorders specialists interchangeable?, *Mov. Disord.*, 20, pp. 1577–1584.

70. Schrag, A., Schelosky, L., Scholz, U. and Poewe, W. (1999). Reduction of parkinsonian signs in patients with Parkinson's disease by dopaminergic versus anticholinergic single-dose challenges, *Mov. Disord.*, 14, pp. 252–255.

71. Keijsers, N. L., Horstink, M. W., van Hilten, J. J., Hoff, J. I. and Gielen, C. C. (2000). Detection and assessment of the severity of levodopa-induced dyskinesia in patients with Parkinson's disease by neural networks, *Mov. Disord.*, 15, pp. 1104–1111.

72. Keijsers, N. L., Horstink, M. W. and Gielen, S. C. (2006). Ambulatory motor assessment in Parkinson's disease, *Mov. Disord.*, 21, pp. 34–44.

73. Gurevich, T. Y., Shabtai, H., Korczyn, A. D., Simon, E. S. and Giladi, N. (2006). Effect of rivastigmine on tremor in patients with Parkinson's disease and dementia, *Mov. Disord.*, 21, pp. 1663–1666.

74. Obwegeser, A. A., Uitti, R. J., Witte, R. J., Lucas, J. A., Turk, M. F. and Wharen, R. E. Jr. (2001). Quantitative and qualitative outcome measures after thalamic deep brain stimulation to treat disabling tremors, *Neurosurgery.*, 48, pp. 274–284.

75. Kumru, H., Summerfield, C., Valldeoriola, F. and Valls-Solé, J. (2004). Effects of subthalamic nucleus stimulation on characteristics of EMG activity underlying reaction time in Parkinson's disease, *Mov. Disord.*, 19, pp. 94–100.

76. Giuffrida, J. P., Riley, D. E., Maddux, B. N. and Heldman, D. A. (2009). Clinically deployable Kinesia™ technology for automated tremor assessment, *Mov. Disord.*, 24, pp. 723–730.

77. Diffraction Limited Design LLC [www.dld-llc.com/Diffraction_Limited_Design_LLC/Vibration.html]

78. LeMoyne, R., Mastroianni, T., Cozza, M., Coroian, C. and Grundfest, W. (2010). Implementation of an iPhone as a wireless accelerometer for quantifying gait characteristics, *Proc. 32nd Annual International Conference of the IEEE, Engineering in Medicine and Biology Society (EMBS)*, pp. 3847–3851.

79. LeMoyne, R., Mastroianni, T. and Grundfest, W. (2011). Wireless accelerometer iPod application for quantifying gait characteristics, *Proc. 33rd Annual International Conference of the IEEE, Engineering in Medicine and Biology Society (EMBS)*, pp. 7904–7907.

80. LeMoyne, R., Mastroianni, T. and Grundfest, W. (2012). Quantified reflex strategy using an iPod as a wireless accelerometer application, *Proc. 34th Annual International Conference of the IEEE, Engineering in Medicine and Biology Society (EMBS)*, pp. 2476–2479.

81. LeMoyne, R., Mastroianni, T., Grundfest, W. and Nishikawa. K. (2013). Implementation of an iPhone wireless accelerometer application for the quantification of reflex response, *Proc.* 35th *Annual International Conference of the IEEE, Engineering in Medicine and Biology Society (EMBS)*, pp. 4658–4661.

82. LeMoyne, R., Kerr, W., Zanjani, K. and Mastroianni, T. (2014). Implementation of an iPod wireless accelerometer application using machine learning to classify disparity of hemiplegic and healthy patellar tendon reflex pair, *J. Med. Imaging Health Inform.*, 4, pp. 21–28.

83. LeMoyne, R., Mastroianni, T. and Montoya, K. (2014). Implementation of a smartphone for evaluating gait characteristics of a trans-tibial prosthesis, *Proc.* 36th *Annual International Conference of the IEEE, Engineering in Medicine and Biology Society (EMBS)*, pp. 3674–3677.

84. LeMoyne, R. and Mastroianni, T. (2014). Implementation of a smartphone as a wireless gyroscope application for the quantification of reflex response, *Proc.* 36th *Annual International Conference of the IEEE, Engineering in Medicine and Biology Society (EMBS)*, pp. 3654–3657.

85. LeMoyne, R. and Mastroianni, T. (2014). Implementation of an iPod application as a wearable and wireless accelerometer system for identifying quantified disparity of hemiplegic gait, *J. Med. Imaging Health Inform.*, 4, pp. 634–641.

86. LeMoyne, R., Kerr, W. and Mastroianni, T. (2015). Implementation of machine learning with an iPod application mounted to cane for classifying assistive device usage, *J. Med. Imaging Health Inform.*, 5, pp. 1404–1408.

87. LeMoyne, R., Mastroianni, T., Hessel, A. and Nishikawa, K. (2015). Ankle rehabilitation system with feedback from a smartphone wireless gyroscope platform and machine learning classification, *Proc. 14th International Conference on Machine Learning and Applications (ICMLA), IEEE*, pp. 406–409.

88. LeMoyne, R., Heerinckx, F., Aranca, T., De Jager, R., Zesiewicz, T. and Saal, H. J. (2016). Wearable body and wireless inertial sensors for

machine learning classification of gait for people with Friedreich's ataxia, *Proc. 13th Annual International Body Sensor Networks Conference (BSN), IEEE*, pp. 147–151.

89. LeMoyne, R. and Mastroianni, T. (2016). Implementation of a smartphone as a wireless gyroscope platform for quantifying reduced arm swing in hemiplegic gait with machine learning classification by multilayer perceptron neural network, *Proc. 38th Annual International Conference of the IEEE, Engineering in Medicine and Biology Society (EMBS)*, pp. 2626–2630.

90. LeMoyne, R. and Mastroianni, T. (2016). Smartphone wireless gyroscope platform for machine learning classification of hemiplegic patellar tendon reflex pair disparity through a multilayer perceptron neural network, *Proc. Wireless Health (WH), IEEE*, pp. 1–6.

91. LeMoyne, R. and Mastroianni, T. (2017). Virtual Proprioception for eccentric training, *Proc. 39th Annual International Conference of the IEEE, Engineering in Medicine and Biology Society (EMBS)*, pp. 4557–4561.

92. LeMoyne, R. and Mastroianni, T. (2017). Wireless gyroscope platform enabled by a portable media device for quantifying wobble board therapy, *Proc. 39th Annual International Conference of the IEEE, Engineering in Medicine and Biology Society (EMBS)*, pp. 2662–2666.

93. LeMoyne, R. and Mastroianni, T. (2017). Implementation of a smartphone wireless gyroscope platform with machine learning for classifying disparity of a hemiplegic patellar tendon reflex pair, *J. Mech. Med. Biol.*, 17, 1750083.

94. LeMoyne, R. and Mastroianni, T. (2017). *Wireless MEMS Networks and Applications*, ed. Uttamchandani, D., Chapter 6 "Wearable and Wireless Gait Analysis Platforms: Smartphones and Portable Media Devices," (Elsevier, New York) pp. 129–152.

95. LeMoyne, R. and Mastroianni, T. (2018). *Wearable and Wireless Systems for Healthcare I: Gait and Reflex Response Quantification*, (Springer, Singapore).

96. LeMoyne, R. and Mastroianni, T. (2018). *Wearable and Wireless Systems for Healthcare I: Gait and Reflex Response Quantification*, Chapter 6 "Smartphones and Portable Media Devices as Wearable and

Wireless Systems for Gait and Reflex Response Quantification," (Springer, Singapore) pp. 73–93.

97. LeMoyne, R. and Mastroianni, T. (2018). *Wearable and Wireless Systems for Healthcare I: Gait and Reflex Response Quantification*, Chapter 10 "Homebound Therapy with Wearable and Wireless Systems," (Springer, Singapore) pp. 121–132.

98. LeMoyne, R. and Mastroianni, T. (2018). Implementation of a smartphone as a wearable and wireless gyroscope platform for machine learning classification of hemiplegic gait through a multilayer perceptron neural network, *Proc. 17th International Conference on Machine Learning and Applications (ICMLA), IEEE*, pp. 946–950.

99. LeMoyne, R. and Mastroianni, T. (2018). *Wearable and Wireless Systems for Healthcare I: Gait and Reflex Response Quantification*, Chapter 9 "Role of Machine Learning for Gait and Reflex Response Classification," (Springer, Singapore) pp. 111–120.

100. Hall, M., Frank, E., Holmes, G., Pfahringer, B., Reutemann, P. and Witten I. H. (2009). The WEKA data mining software: An update, *ACM SIGKDD Explor. Newsl.*, 11, pp. 10–18.

101. Witten, I. H., Frank, E. and Hall, M. A. (2011). *Data Mining: Practical Machine Learning Tools and Techniques*, 3rd Ed. (Morgan Kaufmann Publishers, Burlington).

102. WEKA [www.cs.waikato.ac.nz/~ml/weka]

103. LeMoyne, R. and Mastroianni, T. (2018). *Wearable and Wireless Systems for Healthcare I: Gait and Reflex Response Quantification*, Chapter 11 "Future Perspective of Network Centric Therapy," (Springer, Singapore) pp. 133–134.

104. LeMoyne, R., Mastroianni, T., Whiting, D. and Tomycz, N. (2019). *Wearable and Wireless Systems for Healthcare II: Movement Disorder Evaluation and Deep Brain Stimulation Systems*, Chapter 10 "New Perspectives for Network Centric Therapy for the Treatment of Parkinson's Disease and Essential Tremor," (Springer, Singapore) pp. 127–128.

Chapter 3

Global Algorithm Development

3.1 Introduction

The amalgamation of wearable and wireless systems with machine learning through the implementation of software automation has been advocated and successfully achieved [1–11]. However, in order to realize this objective efficiently, a process for developing the software algorithm is advocated. There are multiple software development processes, such as the waterfall model and incremental development [12]. A central theme to the software development process is the refinement of requirements to better elucidate the overall software objectives [13]. A successful series of requirements are advocated in light of previous software automation to consolidate signal data to a feature set amenable for machine learning classification [14–38]. The establishment of requirements is especially significant for software applied to regulated environments [39].

In order to improve the efficacy, requirements techniques, such as the Fagan inspection, can be implemented [40, 41]. These requirements can be generalized using commenting of the code. Software design, implementation, and testing can then be applied [42, 43]. A further review of the information, such as the acceleration signal, to be read into the software program is recommended [16].

At this phase of development, the pseudo code can be developed, which further specifies the requirements in a more refined manner [44]. The requirements and pseudo code are oriented toward being amenable for the Waikato Environment for Knowledge Analysis

(WEKA), which is a robust machine learning platform [45–47]. Subsequently, programming languages, such as Python, R, and Octave, are relevant for consideration [48–51]. Based on the methodical software development process under consideration, Python has been selected as the programming language of preference.

Upon the later phases of the software development process platforms, such as the Anaconda Distribution and Jupyter Notebook, can be utilized [52, 53]. Appropriate libraries, such as numpy, which is also known as Numerical Python are available for implementation [48, 54–56]. Online resources for Python programming syntax can also facilitate the software development process [49, 57–60].

Respective of the terminal phases of the software development process is the concept of Kaizen. Kaizen is the incorporation of continuous improvement [61, 62]. These observations for the software development process serve to satisfy the objective of this chapter, which is to provide a global perspective for the development of algorithms for software programs.

3.2 Software Development Process

The structure of an organized and precedent derived means for developing software enables an intuitively efficient strategy. The software development process is organized through a series of staged increments that progressively clarifies the objective under consideration. Although the software development process may at first light appear slightly excessive for a small team of talented programmers, its inherent utility is more notable as the team grows in size, the software grows in complexity, and the software becomes more of a candidate for reuse and a subject for historic preservation. In particular, two models for the software development process are the waterfall model and incremental development. Notably, these two models and their application can coexist in tandem for the benefit of the development team [12].

3.3 Waterfall Model

The waterfall model incorporates a series of processes for the development of a software application in discrete increments. In order to

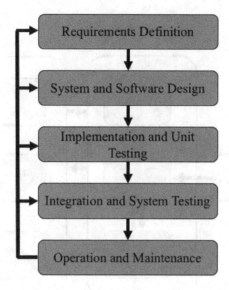

Fig. 3.1. The waterfall model [12].

proceed to the subsequent phase, the current phase is required to be resolved. During the requirements definition phase, the objectives of the software are clearly communicated. For the system and software design aspect, the goal is to assert fundamental software relationships. With these phases of clear communication, the implementation and unit testing is achieved, for which the programing is realized, and unit level testing verifies preliminary satisfaction of the requirements. Subsequently, integration and system testing occurs that involves testing of the cohesive software program to ensure that the amalgamated effect of the requirements have been achieved. During the operation and maintenance phase the software is practically utilized. Corrective interventions are applied to unforeseen error, and enhancement to the software are presented as upgrades. Figure 3.1 presents an illustration of the waterfall model [12].

3.4 Incremental Development

Rather than applying discretely segmented stages, the endeavors of requirements definition, development, and validation are conducted in an interleaved manner. The software is developed in a series of

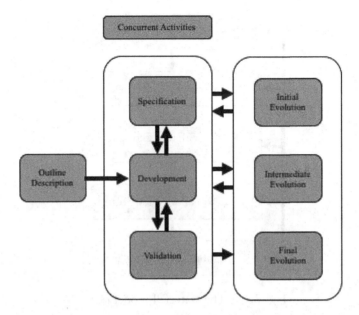

Fig. 3.2.   Incremental development [12].

progressive incremental versions. An advantage of the incremental development software development process relative to the waterfall model, is the reduction of cost for accommodating modifications to the requirements. Figure 3.2 presents an interpretation of the incremental development software development process [12].

3.5 Requirements Definition

The requirements summarize the essence of the general expectations of software program that are in the development process. Respective of functional requirements they elucidate a perspective of the program's implementation. For more sophisticated software process development endeavors the requirements are consolidated into a software requirements document [13]. For the scope of this software objective the following requirements are recommended:

(1) Import the relevant set of libraries for the software program.
(2) Read the acceleration signal data.

(3) Process the acceleration signal data to acquire the acceleration magnitude.

(4) Plot the acceleration magnitude as a function of time.

(5) Consolidate the acceleration magnitude signal data to attributes for the Attribute-Relation File Format (ARFF) feature set.

(6) Write the feature set information to an ARFF file.

These software requirements have been successfully implemented for multiple machine learning classification applications using software automation to consolidate the signal data to a feature set. These requirements especially pertain to wearable and wireless inertial sensor systems using machine learning classification [14–38]. A requirements flowchart is presented in Figure 3.3 for realizing the objective of the software.

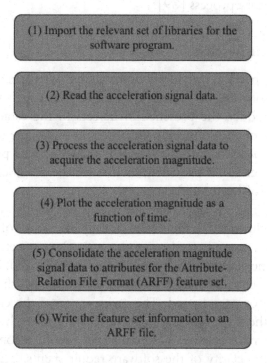

Fig. 3.3.   Requirements flowchart for achieving the software objective.

3.6 Significance of Requirements

Although for preliminary programming endeavors may appear unnecessary, the elucidation of requirements serves the critical role of communicating the intent of software program. The software requirements reflect the design theme of the program. Especially for more complex software consisting of a team of multiple programmers, a clearly communicated set of requirements articulates a decisive pathway for the evolution of the software development process.

The establishment of requirements provides a foundation for the verification that the completed software program satisfies the overall intent and objective of the software development process. The requirements serve an instrumental basis for quality engineering and assurance. Of paramount significance, the documentation of requirements serves a critical role for the Food and Drug Administration (FDA) regulatory process [39].

3.7 Fagan Inspection

The Fagan inspection provides a useful technique for reinforcing the quality of a software development process. The Fagan inspection is intended to reduce the presence of defects in the establishment of requirements for the software program. This technique was provided by Dr. Fagan of IBM during 1976 [40, 41]. A general perspective of the Fagan inspection is provided, such as for the consideration of the foundational software requirements.

There are five essential roles for the team conducting the Fagan inspection as illustrated in Figure 3.4. Ideally the author of the software requirements is present to advocate the author's perspective, especially in the event the clarity of the requirements is challenged. The requirements are sequentially read by the assigned reader, which may be read verbatim and/or paraphrased. The reviewers serve the critical role of interpreting the requirements while evaluating and challenging the clarity of the requirements. The scribe may record recommendations for evolving the clarity of the software requirements. The moderator ensures team cohesion, efficiency, and provisional leadership of the Fagan inspection process. The Fagan inspection technique serves the

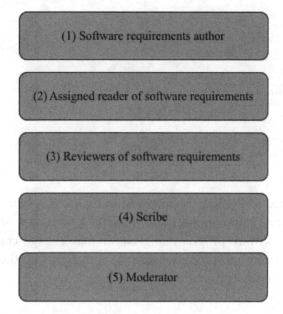

Fig. 3.4.   The five primary roles for the Fagan inspection team [40, 41].

vital role of identifying and mitigating defects regarding the critical requirements phase of the software programming process [40,41].

3.8 The Value of Commenting

Software programming is generally intended for reuse, incremental upgrade, and improvement. The likelihood is considerable that the original authors of a specific software program may not be readily available for the evolutionary application of their code. Therefore, a narrative of the general perspective of the requirements, the intent of the program, the flow of information throughout the program, and the significance of assigned variables is imperative for its sustainability and progressive use of the software. This nonobvious but substantial aspect of software programming is known as commenting.

Commenting is elicited by assigning a specific character before the comment line, such as for Python the number sign (pound sign) '#' is applied. In particular, the quantity of comments instilled into a program does not affect the processing time. For example, the comment line

```
In [ ]: #
        #   This program automates the consolidation of
        #   the accelerometer signal to an ARFF file for
        #   machine learning classification using WEKA.
        #
        #   The experiment involves a reach and grasp
        #   task for a subject with Essential tremor.
        #
        #   Two scenarios are applied. One scenario
        #   involves deep brain stimulation set to 'On'.
        #   The second scenario involves the deep brain
        #   stimulation system set to 'Off'.
        #
        #   The accelerometer signal is recorded through
        #   a smartphone functioning as a wearable and
        #   wireless inertial sensor system.
        #
```

Fig. 3.5.   Commenting lines using Python.

may be applied to Python, as illustrated in Figure 3.5. Notice the commenting involves a preliminary and final blank comment line for readability. The software programming editor may change colors for the benefit of the user upon commencing the comment with the commenting character, such as the '#' for Python.

3.9 Design and Implementation

During the design and implementation phase of the software development process the executable software is developed. The design and implementation are effectively amalgamated. With the requirements properly articulated, the architectural design may be defined with progressive evolution of clarity and specificity. During this process the consideration of design patterns may be considered, which incorporates the problem scenario and its resolution in a manner such that the software may be reused in disparate environments [42].

The pending implementation phase involves the development of executable software. During the implementation phase the incorporation of stable existing code is highly recommended. As the complexity of the software increases, the concept of configuration management becomes more relevant, such as managing the active versions of the evolving software [42].

3.10 Software Testing

The purpose of software testing is to verify that the software achieves the objectives defined by the requirements. Generally, this can be demonstrated using preexisting data. Another benefit of software testing regards ascertaining defects pertaining to the software. The testing process can span the domains of resolving defects, assuring the software satisfies the requirements, and formal evaluation by the presumptive user [43].

3.11 The Comma-Separated Values File Storing the Acceleration Signal Derived from the Vibration Smartphone Application

In order to properly extract the acceleration signal from the Vibration smartphone application's Comma-Separated Values (CSV) file, the contents of the file must be thoroughly addressed. As illustrated in Figure 3.6, the accelerometer signal CSV file acquired from the smartphone Vibration application first consists of a series of header files, which should be bypassed during the reading of the CSV file. Subsequent to the header section and also presented in Figure 3.6 are the columns representing the accelerometer signal data [16].

Observing Figure 3.6, below the header section and proceeding from left to right are four columns of accelerometer signal data. The first column represents time defined by units of seconds. Columns two, three, and four represent the x-, y-, and z-directions of the

```
 1  Vibration iOSApp file: VibrationData 2019-08-11 at 16 23 31-email.csv
 2  Source,Internal Accelerometer
 3  Date and Time,2019-08-11 at 16:23:31
 4  3,  Channels
 5  512, Points
 6  100.000000, Sample Rate (Hz)
 7  -83.382866, Longitude
 8  42.421509, Latitude
 9  0.000000, Speed (m/s)
10  Frequency Data State, Acceleration
11  Time,X,Y,Z
12  0.00000000,-0.01888946,-0.07160609,1.00925529
13  0.01001000,-0.01447306,-0.06851625,1.00684655
14  0.02002000,-0.01513246,-0.06562527,1.00356865
15  0.03003000,-0.01215752,-0.06642067,1.00949919
16  0.04007000,-0.01269423,-0.06808796,1.00744104
17  0.05008000,-0.01686528,-0.06795029,1.00748682
18  0.06008900,-0.01099208,-0.06765967,1.00824904
19  0.07009900,-0.00944327,-0.06307080,1.00521517
20  0.08010900,-0.01542381,-0.06025629,1.00623667
21  0.09014900,-0.01697262,-0.06873040,1.00507796
22  0.10015900,-0.01283225,-0.06811855,1.00262344
23  0.11016900,-0.02132768,-0.06325435,1.00268447
24  0.12017800,-0.02279982,-0.06678778,1.00199842
25  0.13021900,-0.01850609,-0.06639007,1.00550485
26  0.14022800,-0.01951819,-0.06161765,1.00562680
27  0.15023801,-0.01764735,-0.06440157,1.00655687
28  0.16024800,-0.01513246,-0.06686426,1.00558114
29  0.17028800,-0.01537781,-0.06681837,1.00776124
30  0.18029800,-0.01346097,-0.06573234,1.00632811
31  0.19030800,-0.01686528,-0.06640537,1.00417852
```

Fig. 3.6. The preliminary rows of the Vibration smartphone application CSV file with header section and subsequent accelerometer signal data [16].

accelerometer signal, which are orthogonal. The acceleration signal is measured in units of g's of gravity, which is to the equivalence of local terrestrial gravitational acceleration [16].

3.12 Pseudo Code Development

With the software requirements defined, the next step is to develop a series of procedural steps to further refine the software development process. The verbalization of the software program's functionality is also known as pseudo code [44]. The pseudo code to achieve the software requirements and objective is presented below:

(1) This aspect consists of the import section, for which the module objects pertaining to the appropriate libraries are imported into the Python program.

(2) The directory and file name with the essential tremor CSV file recording the acceleration signal, recorded by the smartphone mounted about the dorsum of the hand using the Vibration app, is assigned to the variable file.

(3) Within the module object pertaining to the appropriate library, the read CSV method reads the accelerometer data from the respective CSV file according to the file variable assignment. The preceding header rows of the CSV file are skipped through a method for skipping the header rows. The delimiter is the comma. The nonessential lines of subsequent data after the temporal accelerometer data, which consist of frequency data, are removed.

(4) The time acceleration signal data for essential tremor stored in the dataframe is modified to lists that define the time, x-acceleration signal, y-acceleration signal, and z-acceleration signal.

(5) The acceleration magnitude is calculated based on the square root of the sum of the squares for the x-, y-, and z-acceleration signals.

(6) Plot the time versus acceleration magnitude signal and save the respective plot with appropriate labeling of title and axes.

(7) The signal processing of the acceleration magnitude (accelMag) is applied to derive the numeric attributes to develop the feature

set for machine learning classification through WEKA [45–47]. The numerical attributes are based on:

- Maximum
- Minimum
- Mean
- Standard deviation
- Coefficient of variation

(8) These respective numerical attributes are calculated from their associated methods through the module object pertaining to the appropriate library.

(9) The command to write the ARFF file with the file handle is established and assigned to the same directory associated with the directory and file name for the essential tremor CSV file.

(10) The write method with the file handle object assigns the header aspect of the ARFF file, which includes the definition of the relation, attributes, and classes [45–47].

(11) The attributes representing the maximum, minimum, mean, standard deviation, and coefficient of variation for the acceleration magnitude of the respective acceleration signal are written to the ARFF file with the associated class [45–47].

(12) Close the file.

3.13 Select an Appropriate Programming Language

With the software programming requirements clearly defined, Fagan inspected, and the pseudo code refining the objective of the software endeavor completed, the selection of an appropriate programming language is recommended. Notice the utility of the preliminary clarifying phases of the software development process. This sequential approach avoids the potential of inadvertently selecting a programming language that would not be amenable to efficiently satisfying the requirements. For the scope of this software development process, three programming languages shall be considered:

(1) Python
(2) R
(3) Octave

3.13.1 *Python*

Python is an object-oriented scripting language that was developed by Guido van Rossum from Amsterdam's National Research Institute for Mathematics and Computer Science. The preliminary public release of Python occurred during 1991. Python is a frequently preferred for education and scientific computing applications. Given the utility of Python, it is advancing to become a highly popular programming language throughout the international community. In particular, Python has transcended the R programming language, popularly, for the domain of data-science applications [48]. Python can also be freely acquired, with many online resources [49].

The utility of Python is especially supported by its open source nature, which enables an extensive community to advocate the programming language. Furthermore, a considerably vast number of libraries are available. These libraries enable the capacity to conduct significant endeavors with relatively succinct coding.

3.13.2 *R*

Another widely used programming language is R. This software platform is also free and is capable of generating data visualization and statistical analysis of considerable quality. The particular role of R is for the domain of statistical applications, and R's capabilities can be extended through the inclusion of packages [50].

3.13.3 *Octave*

The Octave scientific programming language with syntax that is resemblant of Matlab. Octave is equipped with an assortment of tools that enables this language for numerical computations. With these capabilities Octave spans the domains of commercial applications, research, and academia [51].

3.14 Selecting the Appropriate Programming Language: Python

Given the consideration of the three available programming languages (Python, R, and Octave) to satisfy the requirement objectives, the selected programming language shall be Python. In particular, Python is a language of rampant growth and expansion. It is equipped with myriad supporting libraries and online resources. Python is especially suitable for the scope of data science, for which the requirement objectives are themed toward the preliminary domain of data science. The application of Python shall be represented by the application of the Anaconda Distribution and Jupyter Notebook.

3.15 Anaconda Distribution and Jupyter Notebook

Python is readily available through the Anaconda Distribution. The Anaconda Distribution is considered one of the most popular platforms for Python pertaining to data science in the world with on the order of 15 million users as of current [52]. The Anaconda Distribution can be downloaded, as of current, through the www. anaconda.com/products/individual homepage by clicking the appropriate download icon.

Intrinsic to the Anaconda Distribution is the Jupyter Notebook [53]. The Jupyter Notebook is presented in Figure 3.7 with respect to the directory structure for accessing executable Python programs.

Fig. 3.7. The folder structure of Jupyter Notebook for accessing executable Python programs.

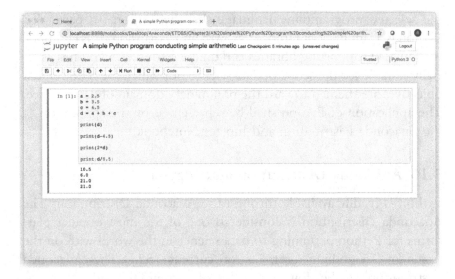

Fig. 3.8.   A simple Python program conducting simple arithmetic, which is executed by clicking the run icon, with the result printed as output.

Figure 3.8 presents a simple Python program that conducts fundamental arithmetic with the result printed as output. The simple Python program is executed through clicking the **Run** icon.

3.16 Relevant Python Libraries

A primary utility of applying Python to resolve the objectives of the requirements is the abundant presence of associated libraries. In particular, there are three Python libraries that are of interest for satisfying the software requirements. These libraries are presented in Figure 3.9.

The numpy library is replete with methods, which makes it uniquely suited for the domains of scientific computing and statistics [48, 54]. The numpy library is also known as Numerical Python. The pandas library pertains to the domains of data manipulation and analysis. The pandas library is popular for the domain of data manipulation, especially in conjunction with the numpy library. The most prevalent data structures are the series, which is one-dimensional, and the

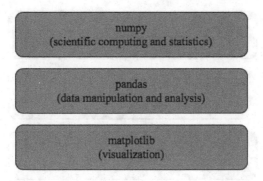

Fig. 3.9. Python libraries and their pertinent roles that are relevant for satisfying the software programming requirements [48, 54].

dataframe, which is two-dimensional. The matplotlib library represents the resources for customizable visualization, such as plotting [48].

A library incorporates an **import** statement to access a module object, such as **import numpy as np**. The numpy library is represented by **np** as the respective module object [54, 55]. With the module object, such as **np**, the desired method is accessed through dot notation. For example, through the numpy library the square of the x-acceleration signal can be attained through **np.square(accelX)** [55, 56].

3.17 Python Online Resources

An intrinsic advantage of utilizing Python as a programming language is the considerable abundance of online resources. Prevalent online resources for Python are featured in Figure 3.10. These online resources can especially resolve matters for clarifying the syntax of the Python programming language.

The www.python.org homepage is supported by the Python Software Foundation, and this homepage is equipped with numerous documentation, which is especially relevant for people new to programming [49]. The www.numpy.org homepage features the scientific computing library for Python, and this homepage is also equipped with considerable documentation [57]. The www.github.com and

Fig. 3.10.   Online resources for mastering Python [49, 57–60].

www.github.com/numpy consist of a repository for software programs, such as for Python, that is especially oriented to version control, which is an aspect of software configuration management [58, 59]. Another online resource is www.stackoverflow.com, which is particularly relevant toward mastering syntax and resolving syntax-oriented errors in coding [60]. Another strategy to access online resources involves entering the topic of concern, syntax error, or the desired software effect using a Google search.

3.18 Additional Concept: Kaizen

Kaizen is a perspective that can substantially impact the quality and efficacy of a software programming endeavor. The term Kaizen is from the Japanese language, and its associated kanji is illustrated in Figure 3.11. The Japanese to English translation for Kaizen is 'kai' meaning 'change' and 'zen' meaning 'for the better' [61].

Fig. 3.11.   Japanese kanji for Kaizen.

The process of Kaizen incorporates progressively incremental improvements to enhance the efficiency and quality of the endeavor under consideration [62]. This concept is highly relevant to the advancement of the software development process. Intuitively, a software program can be progressively evolved, and the application of Kaizen can substantially improve the software under consideration over a long-range timeframe.

3.19 Conclusion

Chapter 2 'General Concept of Preliminary Network Centric Therapy Applying Deep Brain Stimulation for Ameliorating Movement Disorders with Machine Learning Classification using Python Based on Feedback from a Smartphone as a Wearable and Wireless System' defines a clear objective. The objective is to apply machine learning classification to distinguish deep brain stimulation set to 'On' and 'Off' status for a subject with essential tremor through objectively quantified feedback, based on the accelerometer signal of a smartphone constituting a wearable and wireless system utilizing Python software automation for conducting post-processing. In order to effectively utilize the capabilities of wearable and wireless systems with the application of machine learning software, automation for post-processing the signal data to a feature set is imperative. In order to achieve this task, the incorporation of a software development processes, such as the waterfall model and incremental development, are recommended.

Inherent to the software development process is the establishment of requirements. The efficacy of the requirements can be augmented through strategies, such as the Fagan inspection. Subsequently, pseudo code can be established. The requirements and pseudo code are guided for being amenable with the operation of WEKA for machine learning classification.

At this stage of the software development process multiple software programming languages, such as Python, R, and Octave, are considered. Python is considered the most appropriate software programming language with the Jupyter Notebook. Additional phases are addressed, such as the concept of Kaizen, which applies the perspective of continuous improvement. With the establishment of requirements and pseudo code, Chapter 4 'Incremental Software Development using Python' proceeds to the incorporation of Python syntax to satisfy the defined objective.

References

1. LeMoyne, R., Coroian, C., Mastroianni, T., Opalinski, P., Cozza, M. and Grundfest, W. (2009). *Biomedical Engineering*, ed. Barros de Mello, C. A., Chapter 10 "The Merits of Artificial Proprioception, with Applications in Biofeedback Gait Rehabilitation Concepts and Movement Disorder Characterization," (InTech, Vienna) pp. 165–198.
2. LeMoyne, R. and Mastroianni, T. (2015). *Mobile Health Technologies, Methods and Protocols*, eds. Rasooly, A. and Herold, K. E., Chapter 23 "Use of Smartphones and Portable Media Devices for Quantifying Human Movement Characteristics of Gait, Tendon Reflex Response, and Parkinson's Disease Hand Tremor," (Springer, New York) pp. 335–358.

3. LeMoyne, R. and Mastroianni, T. (2016). *Telemedicine*, "Telemedicine Perspectives for Wearable and Wireless Applications Serving the Domain of Neurorehabilitation and Movement Disorder Treatment," (SMGroup, Dover) pp. 1–10.

4. LeMoyne, R. and Mastroianni, T. (2017). *Wireless MEMS Networks and Applications*, ed. Uttamchandani, D., Chapter 6 "Wearable and Wireless Gait Analysis Platforms: Smartphones and Portable Media Devices," (Elsevier, New York) pp. 129–152.

5. LeMoyne, R. and Mastroianni, T. (2017). *Smartphones from an Applied Research Perspective*, ed. Mohamudally, N., Chapter 1 "Smartphone and Portable Media Device: A Novel Pathway Toward the Diagnostic Characterization of Human Movement," (InTech, Rijeka) pp. 1–24.

6. LeMoyne, R. and Mastroianni, T. (2018). *Wearable and Wireless Systems for Healthcare I: Gait and Reflex Response Quantification*, (Springer, Singapore).

7. LeMoyne, R. and Mastroianni, T. (2018). *Wearable and Wireless Systems for Healthcare I: Gait and Reflex Response Quantification*, Chapter 9 "Role of Machine Learning for Gait and Reflex Response Classification," (Springer, Singapore) pp. 111–120.

8. LeMoyne, R., Mastroianni, T., Whiting, D. and Tomycz, N. (2019). *Wearable and Wireless Systems for Healthcare II: Movement Disorder Evaluation and Deep Brain Stimulation Systems*, (Springer, Singapore).

9. LeMoyne, R., Mastroianni, T., Whiting, D. and Tomycz, N. (2019). *Wearable and Wireless Systems for Healthcare II: Movement Disorder Evaluation and Deep Brain Stimulation Systems*, Chapter 8, "Role of Machine Learning for Classification of Movement Disorder and Deep Brain Stimulation Status," (Springer, Singapore) pp. 99–111.

10. LeMoyne, R. and Mastroianni, T. (2019). *Smartphones: Recent Innovations and Applications*, ed. Dabove, P., Chapter 7 "Network Centric Therapy for Wearable and Wireless Systems," (Nova Science Publishers, Hauppauge).

11. LeMoyne, R. and Mastroianni, T. (2020). *Multilayer Perceptrons: Theory and Applications*, ed. Vang-Mata, R., Chapter 2, "Machine Learning Classification for Network Centric Therapy Utilizing the Multilayer Perceptron Neural Network," (Nova Science Publishers, Hauppauge) pp. 39–76.

12. Sommerville, I. (2011). *Software Engineering*, 9th Ed., Chapter 2 "Software Processes," (Addison Wesley, New York) pp. 27–55.

13. Sommerville, I. (2011). *Software Engineering*, 9th Ed., Chapter 4 "Requirements Engineering," (Addison Wesley, New York) pp. 82–117.

14. LeMoyne, R., Kerr, W., Zanjani, K. and Mastroianni, T. (2014). Implementation of an iPod wireless accelerometer application using machine learning to classify disparity of hemiplegic and healthy patellar tendon reflex pair, *J. Med. Imaging Health Inform.*, 4, pp. 21–28.

15. LeMoyne, R., Kerr, W., Mastroianni, T. and Hessel, A. (2014). Implementation of machine learning for classifying hemiplegic gait disparity through use of a force plate, *Proc. 13th International Conference on Machine Learning and Applications (ICMLA), IEEE*, pp. 379–382.

16. LeMoyne, R., Tomycz, N., Mastroianni, T., McCandless, C., Cozza, M. and Peduto, D. (2015). Implementation of a smartphone wireless accelerometer platform for establishing deep brain stimulation treatment efficacy of essential tremor with machine learning, *Proc. 37th Annual International Conference of the IEEE, Engineering in Medicine and Biology Society (EMBS)*, pp. 6772–6775.

17. LeMoyne, R., Mastroianni, T., Hessel, A. and Nishikawa, K. (2015). Implementation of machine learning for classifying prosthesis type through conventional gait analysis, *Proc. 37th Annual International Conference of the IEEE, Engineering in Medicine and Biology Society (EMBS)*, pp. 202–205.

18. LeMoyne, R. and Mastroianni, T. (2015). Machine learning classification of a hemiplegic and healthy patellar tendon reflex pair through an iPod wireless gyroscope platform, *Proc. 45th Society for Neuroscience Annual Meeting*.

19. LeMoyne, R., Kerr, W. and Mastroianni, T. (2015). Implementation of machine learning with an iPod application mounted to cane for classifying assistive device usage, *J. Med. Imaging Health Inform.*, 5, pp. 1404–1408.

20. LeMoyne, R., Mastroianni, T., Hessel, A. and Nishikawa, K. (2015). Application of a multilayer perceptron neural network for classifying software platforms of a powered prosthesis through a force plate, *Proc. 14th International Conference on Machine Learning and Applications (ICMLA), IEEE*, pp. 402–405.

21. LeMoyne, R., Mastroianni, T., Hessel, A. and Nishikawa, K. (2015). Ankle rehabilitation system with feedback from a smartphone wireless gyroscope platform and machine learning classification, *Proc. 14th International Conference on Machine Learning and Applications (ICMLA), IEEE*, pp. 406–409.

22. LeMoyne, R., Heerinckx, F., Aranca, T., De Jager, R., Zesiewicz, T. and Saal, H. J. (2016). Wearable body and wireless inertial sensors for machine learning classification of gait for people with Friedreich's ataxia, *Proc. 13th Annual International Body Sensor Networks Conference (BSN), IEEE*, pp. 147–151.

23. LeMoyne, R. and Mastroianni, T. (2016). Implementation of a smartphone as a wireless gyroscope platform for quantifying reduced arm swing in hemiplegic gait with machine learning classification by multilayer perceptron neural network, *Proc. 38th Annual International Conference of the IEEE, Engineering in Medicine and Biology Society (EMBS)*, pp. 2626–2630.

24. LeMoyne, R. and Mastroianni, T. (2016). Smartphone wireless gyroscope platform for machine learning classification of hemiplegic patellar tendon reflex pair disparity through a multilayer perceptron neural network, *Proc. Wireless Health (WH), IEEE*, pp. 1–6.

25. LeMoyne, R. and Mastroianni, T. (2016). Implementation of a multilayer perceptron neural network for classifying a hemiplegic and healthy reflex pair using an iPod wireless gyroscope platform, *Proc. 46th Society for Neuroscience Annual Meeting*.

26. LeMoyne, R. and Mastroianni, T. (2017). Virtual proprioception for eccentric training, *Proc. 39th Annual International Conference of the IEEE, Engineering in Medicine and Biology Society (EMBS)*, pp. 4557–4561.

27. LeMoyne, R. and Mastroianni, T. (2017). Wireless gyroscope platform enabled by a portable media device for quantifying wobble board therapy, *Proc. 39th Annual International Conference of the IEEE, Engineering in Medicine and Biology Society (EMBS)*, pp. 2662–2666.

28. LeMoyne, R. and Mastroianni, T. (2017). Implementation of a smartphone wireless gyroscope platform with machine learning for classifying disparity of a hemiplegic patellar tendon reflex pair, *J. Mech. Med. Biol.*, 17, 1750083.

29. LeMoyne, R., Mastroianni, T., Tomycz, N., Whiting, D., Oh, M., McCandless, C., Currivan, C. and Peduto, D. (2017). Implementation of a multilayer perceptron neural network for classifying deep brain stimulation in 'On' and 'Off' modes through a smartphone representing a wearable and wireless sensor application, *Proc. 47th Society for Neuroscience Annual Meeting, featured in Hot Topics (top 1% of abstracts)*.

30. LeMoyne, R., Mastroianni, T., McCandless, C., Currivan, C., Whiting, D. and Tomycz, N. (2018). Implementation of a smartphone as a wearable and wireless accelerometer and gyroscope platform for ascertaining deep brain stimulation treatment efficacy of Parkinson's disease through machine learning classification, *Adv. Park. Dis.*, 7, pp. 19–30.

31. LeMoyne, R., Mastroianni, T., McCandless, C., Currivan, C., Whiting, D. and Tomycz, N. (2018). Implementation of a smartphone as a wearable and wireless inertial sensor platform for determining efficacy of deep brain stimulation for Parkinson's disease tremor through machine learning, *Proc. 48th Society for Neuroscience Annual Meeting, Nanosymposium*.

32. LeMoyne, R. and Mastroianni, T. (2018). Implementation of a smartphone as a wearable and wireless gyroscope platform for machine learning classification of hemiplegic gait through a multilayer perceptron neural network, *Proc. 17th International Conference on Machine Learning and Applications (ICMLA), IEEE*, pp. 946–950.

33. LeMoyne, R., Mastroianni, T., Whiting, D. and Tomycz, N. (2019). *Wearable and Wireless Systems for Healthcare II: Movement Disorder Evaluation and Deep Brain Stimulation Systems*, Chapter 9, "Assessment of Machine Learning Classification Strategies for the Differentiation of Deep Brain Stimulation "On" and "Off" Status for Parkinson's Disease Using a Smartphone as a Wearable and Wireless Inertial Sensor for Quantified Feedback," (Springer, Singapore) pp. 113–126.

34. LeMoyne, R., Mastroianni, T., McCandless, C., Whiting, D. and Tomycz, N. (2019). Evaluation of machine learning algorithms for classifying deep brain stimulation respective of 'On' and 'Off' status, *Proc. 9th International IEEE Conference on Neural Engineering (NER), IEEE/EMBS*, pp. 483–488.

35. LeMoyne, R. and Mastroianni, T. (2019). Classification of software control architectures for a powered prosthesis through conventional gait

analysis using machine learning applications, *J. Mech. Med. Biol.*, 19, 1950044.

36. LeMoyne, R., Mastroianni, T., Whiting, D. and Tomycz, N. (2019). Network Centric Therapy for deep brain stimulation status parametric analysis with machine learning classification, *Proc. 49th Society for Neuroscience Annual Meeting, Nanosymposium.*

37. LeMoyne, R., Mastroianni, T., Whiting, D. and Tomycz, N. (2019). Preliminary Network Centric Therapy for machine learning classification of deep brain stimulation status for the treatment of Parkinson's disease with a conformal wearable and wireless inertial sensor, *Adv. Park. Dis.*, 8, pp. 75–91.

38. Mastroianni, T. and LeMoyne, R. (2016). Application of a multilayer perceptron neural network with an iPod as a wireless gyroscope platform to classify reduced arm swing gait for people with Erb's palsy, *Proc. 46th Society for Neuroscience Annual Meeting.*

39. Food and Drug Administration. (2002). *General Principles of Software Validation; Final Guidance for Industry and FDA Staff,* (Food and Drug Administration, Rockville).

40. Fagan, M. E. (1986). Advances in software inspections, *IEEE Trans. Softw. Eng.*, SE-12, pp. 744–751.

41. Fagan, M. E. (1999). Design and code inspections to reduce errors in program development, *IBM Syst. J.*, 38, pp. 258–287.

42. Sommerville, I. (2011). *Software Engineering*, 9th Ed., Chapter 7 "Design and Implementation," (Addison Wesley, New York) pp. 176–204.

43. Sommerville, I. (2011). *Software Engineering*, 9th Ed., Chapter 8 "Software Testing," (Addison Wesley, New York) pp. 205–233.

44. Deitel, H. M., Deitel P. J., Nieto T. R. and McPhie D. C. (2001). *Perl: How to Program*, Chapter 3 "Control Structures: Part I," (Prentice Hall, Upper Saddle River) pp. 60–93.

45. Hall, M., Frank, E., Holmes, G., Pfahringer, B., Reutemann, P. and Witten I. H. (2009). The WEKA data mining software: An update, *ACM SIGKDD Explor. Newsl.*, 11, pp. 10–18.

46. Witten, I. H., Frank, E. and Hall, M. A. (2011). *Data Mining: Practical Machine Learning Tools and Techniques*, 3rd Ed. (Morgan Kaufmann Publishers, Burlington).

47. WEKA [www.cs.waikato.ac.nz/~ml/weka/]

48. Deitel, H. and Deitel, P. (2019). *Python for Programmers with Introductory AI Case Studies,* Chapter 1 "Introduction to Computers and Python," (Prentice Hall, New York) pp. 1–30.
49. Python [www.python.org]
50. R [www.r-project.org/about.html]
51. Octave [www.gnu.org/software/octave/about.html]
52. Anaconda [www.anaconda.com/products/individual]
53. Jupyter [www.jupyter.org/install]
54. Quick Start for Numpy [www.numpy.org/devdocs/user/quickstart. html]
55. Severance, C. (2013). *Python for Informatics: Exploring Information,* Chapter 4 "Functions," (CreateSpace) pp. 43–56.
56. numpy.square [www.numpy.org/doc/stable/reference/generated/ numpy.square.html]
57. Numpy [www.numpy.org]
58. GitHub [www.github.com]
59. GitHub for Numpy [www.github.com/numpy]
60. Stackoverflow [www.stackoverflow.com]
61. Kaizen [www.kaizen.com]
62. Kaizen Glossary [www.kaizen.com/learn-kaizen/glossary.html]

Chapter 4

Incremental Software Development using Python

4.1 Introduction

The software development process applies the further evolution of integrating the established requirements with pseudo code of enhanced refinement for the global objective of developing software to extract inertial sensor signal data in an automated context. These stages of the software development process enable the motivational clarification of the intent of the automation software [1, 2]. In order to satisfy the requirements, Python has been selected as the most appropriate programing language [3–5]. These requirements are derived from the successful advocation and implementation of software programming techniques for consolidating signal data into a feature set amenable for machine learning using the Waikato Environment for Knowledge Analysis (WEKA) [6–44].

The subsequent phase emphasizes implementation of the software program [45]. Upon reaching this stage of the software development process incremental conversion of the requirements and pseudo code to actual Python syntax using the Jupyter Notebook is demonstrated. The relevant Python syntax is presented to achieve the requirements [1–5, 45, 46].

The preliminary implementation phase is accompanied by testing and evaluation [47]. Testing and evaluation of the developed software reveal the presence of a signal anomaly. With this issue revealed through the preliminary software testing and evaluation, provisional Python coding is applied to ameliorate the signal anomaly.

4.2 Review Requirements with Pseudo Code Interleaved

As the themes of Chapter 3 'Global Algorithm Development' infer, the software development process strongly emphasizes the imperative need for clearly articulating expectations. Prior the incremental development of actual Python software with syntax, the requirements and associated pseudo code shall be amalgamated [1–5]. This amalgamation is comprised of six requirements and 12 pseudo code descriptions. Therefore, some of the requirements apply one pseudo code description, and other requirements encapsulate multiple pseudo code descriptions.

The first requirement organizes the libraries for the Python program:

Requirement 1: Import the relevant set of libraries for the software program.

In order to achieve Requirement 1, the first pseudo code description is applied:

Pseudo code 1: The section consists of the import section, for which the module objects pertaining to the appropriate libraries are imported into the Python program.

The second requirement involves reading the acceleration signal data:

Requirement 2: Read this acceleration signal data.

Since Requirement 2 is intuitively complex, this requirement utilized three aspects of pseudo code to satisfy the requirement:

Pseudo code 2: The directory and file name with the essential tremor Comma-Separated Values (CSV) file recording the acceleration signal recorded by the smartphone mounted about the dorsum of the hand using the Vibration app are assigned to the variable file.

Pseudo code 3: Within the module object pertaining to the appropriate library the read_csv method reads the accelerometer data from the respective CSV file according to the file variable assignment. The preceding header rows of the CSV file are skipped through skiprows. The delimiter is the comma. The nonessential lines of subsequent data after the temporal accelerometer data, which consist of frequency data, are removed.

Pseudo code 4: The time acceleration signal data for essential tremor stored in the dataframe is modified to lists that define the time, x-acceleration signal, y-acceleration signal, and z-acceleration signal.

With Requirement 2 realized, the resolution of Requirement 3 is effectively straight forward.

Requirement 3: Process the acceleration signal data to acquire the acceleration magnitude.

The associated pseudo code for Requirement 3 is attained through calculating the acceleration magnitude based on the orthogonal axes of the accelerometer.

Pseudo code 5: The acceleration magnitude is calculated based on the square root of the sum of the squares for the x, y, and z acceleration signals.

With the post-processing of the accelerometer signal Requirement 4 asserts the need to visualize the acceleration magnitude.

Requirement 4: Plot the acceleration magnitude as a function of time.

Further evolution of Requirement 4 is provided by labeling and saving the respective plot.

Pseudo code 6: Plot the time versus acceleration magnitude signal and save the respective plot with appropriate labeling of title and axes.

The acceleration signal data must be consolidated into a feature set with numeric attributes through Requirement 5:

Requirement 5: Consolidate the acceleration magnitude signal data to attributes for the Attribute-Relation File Format (ARFF) feature set.

The achievement of Requirement 5 is attained through the application of descriptive statistics respective of the acceleration magnitude, which is achieved by two pseudo code descriptions.

Pseudo code 7: The signal processing of the acceleration magnitude (accelMag) is applied to derive the numeric attribute to develop the feature set for machine learning classification through WEKA. The numerical attributes are based on the maximum, minimum, mean, standard deviation, and coefficient of variation.

Pseudo code 8: These respective numerical attributes are calculated from their associated methods through the module object pertaining to the appropriate library.

The final aspects of the software program are provided by Requirement 6, which involves assigning the attributes of the feature set to an ARFF file.

Requirement 6: Write the feature set information to an ARFF file.

The satisfaction of Requirement 6 is provided through the consideration of four pseudo code descriptions.

Pseudo code 9: The command to write the ARFF file with the file handle is established and assigned to the same directory associated with the directory and file name for the essential tremor CSV file.

Pseudo code 10: The write method with the file handle object assigns the header aspect of the ARFF file, which includes the definition of the relation, attributes, and classes.

Pseudo code 11: The attributes representing the maximum, minimum, mean, standard deviation, and coefficient of variation for the acceleration magnitude of the respective acceleration signal are written to the ARFF file with the associated class.

Pseudo code 12: Close the file.

Essentially, these software requirements and associated pseudo code been applied for multiple machine learning classification applications that incorporate software automation to post-process the signal data to a feature set. These software requirements and pseudo code are highly relevant for wearable and wireless inertial sensor systems utilizing machine learning classification [6–44].

4.3 Incremental Conversion of Requirements and Pseudo Code to Python Syntax

The next aspect of realizing the software development process involves the conversion of requirements and associated pseudo code to the appropriate Python syntax [1–5, 45]. In particular, the preceding requirements and pseudo code may be applied to any other software language, such as R and Octave, at the software development teams discretion. During this phase, the use of Internet searching may particularly facilitate the process. Furthermore, the pseudo code descriptions may be modified to suit the role of commenting throughout the software program.

The first phase involves the selection of the appropriate libraries for the software program. These libraries are discussed in Chapter 3 'Global Algorithm Development'. The **import** statement acquires the library, and for the purpose of readability the library may be reduced to a textually smaller module object using the **as** statement. Figure 4.1 illustrates the Python syntax using the Jupyter Notebook for Requirement 1 of the software program.

Subsequently, the multiple pseudo code descriptions for Requirement 2 are transformed to appropriate Python syntax. In particular the **file** variable simplifies the software for accessing the respective CSV file. Figure 4.2 presents the definition of the respective CSV file and associated commenting.

```
In [ ]: #
        #   The section consists of the import section, for which the modules objects: numpy, matplotlib, matplotlib.pyplot,
        #   and pandas are imported into the Python program.  The numpy module is assigned to np.  The matplotlib module
        #   retains its original name, and the matplotlib.pyplot is assigned to plt.  The pandas module is assigned to pd.
        #

        import numpy as np
        import matplotlib
        import matplotlib.pyplot as plt
        import pandas as pd
```

Fig. 4.1. The recommended Python syntax and commenting for satisfying Requirement 1 using the Jupyter Notebook.

```
In [ ]: #
        #  The directory and file name with the Essential tremor CSV file recording the acceleration recorded by the
        #  smartphone mounted about the dorsum of the hand using the Vibration application is assigned to the variable file.
        #
        file = 'On/VibrationData 2015-01-27 at 15 49 00-email.csv'
```

Fig. 4.2. The Python syntax and commenting defining the CSV file through the Jupyter Notebook.

```
In [ ]: #
        #  Within the pandas (assigned as pd) module object the read_csv method reads the accelerometer data from the
        #  respective CSV file according to the file variable assignment.  The first nine header rows of the CSV file
        #  are skipped through skiprows.  The delimiter is the comma.  The 260 lines of subsequent data after the
        #  temporal accelerometer data, which consists of frequency data, are removed.  The parser engine is defined
        #  as Python.  The 10th row defines each column in the dataframe.
        #
        columns = pd.read_csv(file, skiprows=[0,1,2,3,4,5,6,7,8], delimiter=',', skipfooter=260, engine='python')
```

Fig. 4.3. The Python syntax and commenting for reading the CSV file using the Jupyter Notebook.

```
In [ ]: #
        #  The acceleration signal data for Essential tremor stored in the dataframe is modified to lists that define
        #  the time, x-acceleration signal, y-acceleration signal, and z-acceleration signal.
        #
        time=columns.Time
        accelX=columns.X
        accelY=columns.Y
        accelZ=columns.Z
```

Fig. 4.4. Python syntax and commenting for reassigning the accelerometer signal for more simplified numerical computation using the Jupyter Notebook.

With the Pandas library the next aspect of Requirement 2 is satisfied. Using **pd** as the module object for Pandas, the **read_csv** method is applied. The **read_csv** method incorporates the **file** variable. Nine header rows are bypassed through **skiprows**. The **delimiter** is defined as the comma. The frequency aspect of the CSV file is bypassed by setting **skipfooter** to 260 rows, and the respective **engine** is defined as Python. Figure 4.3 presents the reading of the CSV file with commenting.

The final aspect of resolving Requirement 2 pertains to redefining the data acquired by incorporating the Pandas library. For simplicity of further numerical computation these aspects of the acceleration signal data are defined as **time**, **accelX**, **accelY**, and **accelZ**. Figure 4.4 displays the Python syntax for assigning the data in a manner more amenable for further numeric computational processing.

```
In [ ]:  #
         #  The numpy module defined as np acquires the acceleration magnitude based on the square root of the sum
         #  of the squares for the x, y, z acceleration signals.
         #
         accelMag=np.sqrt(np.square(accelX) + np.square(accelY) + np.square(accelZ))
```

Fig. 4.5.   The numerical computation for achieving Requirement 3 through Python syntax and commenting using Jupyter Notebook.

The derivation of the acceleration magnitude is achieved through Requirement 3. During this phase the **numpy** library is utilized with the module object assigned as **np**. The acceleration magnitude is computed as the square root for the sum of the squares for the orthogonal (x, y, and z) axes of the accelerometer. In order to achieve the computation of the acceleration magnitude, two methods are utilized: **square** for squaring each acceleration signal and **sqrt** for taking the square root for the respective sum of the squares. The numerical computation process to satisfy Requirement 3 is presented in Figure 4.5.

With the post-processing satisfied, Requirement 4 serves the critical aspect of visualizing the acceleration magnitude as a function of time in the form of a plot with defined axes and title. The matplotlib library and matplotlib.pyplot utilizes the module object **plt**. The method **subplots** assigns **fig** and **ax**. The **plot** method graphs the accelMag (acceleration magnitude) as a function of time.

Matplotlib **ax** axes object regulates the content presented in the respective window. The axes' object consists of a method **set** that applies the string within the parentheses centered and above the plot. The **set** method for the **ax** axes object defines the **xlabel** text for the x-axis, the **ylabel** text for the y-label, and the **title** text [46].

The subsequent methods pertain to the visualization and storage of the plot. The **savefig** method stored the visualization of the graph. The **show** method presents the labeled graph within the Jupyter Notebook. The process for satisfying Requirement 4 is represented in Figure 4.6

With the visualization of the accelerometer signal satisfied the Requirement 5 involves the signal processing of the acceleration magnitude signal into five numerical attributes: maximum, minimum, mean, standard deviation, and coefficient of variation. The **np** module

```
In [ ]:  #
         #    The time vs. acceleration magnitude signal is plotted, and the respective plot is saved with
         #    appropriate labeling of title and axes.
         #

         fig, ax = plt.subplots()
         ax.plot(time, accelMag)

         ax.set(xlabel='Time (s)', ylabel='Acceleration (g\'s)',
                title='Acceleration magnitude as a function of time')

         fig.savefig("TimeAccelMag.png")
         plt.show()
```

Fig. 4.6. The Python syntax and commenting for producing graphical presentation of the acceleration magnitude as a function of time through the Jupyter Notebook.

```
In [ ]:  #
         #    The signal processing of the acceleration magnitude (accelMag) is applied to derive the numeric attributes to
         #    develop the feature set for machine learning classification through Waikato Environment for Knowledge
         #    Analysis (WEKA).  The numeric attributes are based on the maximum, minimum, mean, standard deviation, and
         #    coefficient of variation.  These respective numeric attributes are calculated from their associated methods
         #    through the numpy module defined as np module object.
         #

         Amag_max=max(accelMag)
         Amag_min=min(accelMag)
         Amag_mean=np.mean(accelMag)
         Amag_stdev=np.std(accelMag)
         Amag_CV=Amag_stdev/Amag_mean
```

Fig. 4.7. The acquisition of the numeric attributes for the feature set through Python syntax and commenting for deriving descriptive statistics of the acceleration magnitude signal as presented by Jupyter Notebook.

object incorporates four methods **max**, **min**, **mean**, and **std** that represent the maximum, minimum, mean, and standard deviation of the acceleration magnitude signals. The coefficient of variation is based on the standard deviation divided by the mean. The Python syntax for achieving these numerical computations and associated commenting is presented in Figure 4.7.

The final aspect of the preliminary Python software program is defined by Requirement 6. The appropriate file handle is assigned, and the numerical attributes derived from the acceleration magnitude signal are written to the ARFF file. In addition, the header section is written to the ARFF file. The output file is then closed. The **fout** file handle is assigned using the **open** method for writing (**'w'**) and assigned to the appropriate directory as presented in Figure 4.8.

With the file handle properly assigned, the next step is to write the proper header section for the ARFF file. The ARFF file is more

```
In [ ]:   #
          #   The command to write the Attribute-Relation File Format (ARFF) with the fout file handle is established and
          #   assigned to the same directory associated with the directory and file name for the Essential tremor CSV file.
          #

          fout = open('On/TimeAccelMag.arff', 'w')
```

Fig. 4.8.   The preliminary Python syntax and commenting for defining the output of numerical attributes for the ARFF file using the Jupyter Notebook.

```
In [ ]:   #
          #   The write method with the file handle object assigns the header aspect of the ARFF file.  Note the definition
          #   of the @relation TimeAccelMag at the top aspect of the ARFF file.  Subsequently, the @attribute defines Amag_max,
          #   Amag_min, Amag_mean, Amag_stdev, and Amag_CV for the maximum, minimum, mean, standard deviation, and coefficient
          #   of variation for the acceleration magnitude of the respective acceleration signal.  Furthermore, the @attribute
          #   defines the 'On' and 'Off' classes.
          #

          fout.write('@relation TimeAccelMag\n\n')
          fout.write('@attribute Amag_max numeric\n')
          fout.write('@attribute Amag_min numeric\n')
          fout.write('@attribute Amag_mean numeric\n')
          fout.write('@attribute Amag_stdev numeric\n')
          fout.write('@attribute Amag_CV numeric\n')
          fout.write('@attribute class {On}\n')
          fout.write('@attribute class {Off}\n\n')
```

Fig. 4.9.   The Python syntax and commenting for writing the ARFF file header to the output file through the Jupyter Notebook.

detailed in pending Chapter 5 'Automation of Feature Set Extraction using Python'. The **write** method is applied with the **fout** file handle to write the '@relation' header, five '@attribute' defining the five numeric attributes (maximum, minimum, mean, standard deviation, and coefficient of variation), and two '@attribute' classes defining the two classes (On and Off). Note the **\n** symbol represents a carriage return. The Python syntax and associated commenting for achieving this aspect of Requirement 6 is presented in Figure 4.9.

The final aspect to satisfy Requirement 6 is to write the five numeric attributes (maximum, minimum, mean, standard deviation, and coefficient of variation) with the associated class to the assigned file. This goal is achieved through the **write** method with the **fout** file handle. The five numeric attribute variables are assigned to the write method through the format operator **%g**, which formats a floating-point number to a string. Subsequently, the **close** method is utilized to close the **fout** file handle. The Python syntax and associated commenting for satisfying the remainder of Requirement 6 is presented in Figure 4.10.

```
In [ ]:  #
         #  The Amag_max, Amag_min, Amag_mean, Amag_stdev, and Amag_CV for the maximum, minimum, mean, standard deviation,
         #  and coefficient of variation for the acceleration magnitude of the respective acceleration signal are written
         #  to the ARFF file with the associated 'On' class.
         #

         fout.write('%g,%g,%g,%g,%g,On\n' % (Amag_max,Amag_min,Amag_mean,Amag_stdev,Amag_CV))

         #
         #  The file is finally closed.
         #

         fout.close()
```

Fig. 4.10. The Python syntax and commenting for writing the numeric attributes to the assigned output file followed by closing the output file handle using the Jupyter Notebook.

4.4 Preliminary Testing and Evaluation of the Python Software

The preliminary version of the software program using Python for post-processing the CSV file comprising the accelerometer signal of a subject with essential tremor using deep brain stimulation has been developed. The program visualizes the acceleration magnitude as a function of time and writes the numerical attributes of the maximum, minimum, mean, standard of deviation, and coefficient of variation consolidated from the acceleration magnitude signal to a preliminary version of the ARFF file with the appropriate header. Given the current stage of the software development process, the preliminary software should be tested and evaluated [47].

Figure 4.11 displays the software program using the Jupyter Notebook, for which the **Run** icon executes the program. Upon successfully running a TimeAccelMag.arff and TimeAccelMag.png are generated for the respective trial. However, upon inspection of the TimeAccelMag.png as presented in Figure 4.12, there apparently is an anomaly in the accelerometer signal data. One point in the data signal stream generates a zero acceleration point. Given this predicament, the theme of Kaizen for continuous improvement should be applied.

In order to resolve this matter, a 'for' loop to screen the data should be inserted between Requirement 3 and Requirement 4. The objective of the 'for' loop shall be to loop through the acceleration magnitude signal and apply a Boolean conditional statement to

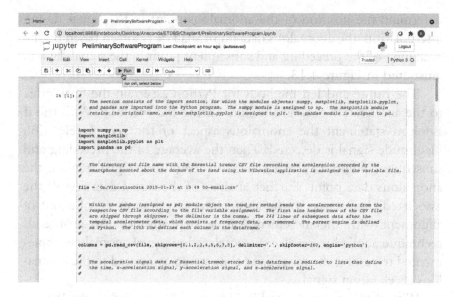

Fig. 4.11. Execution of the preliminary software program through the Jupyter Notebook.

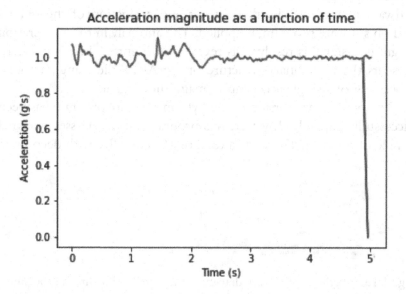

Fig. 4.12. The acceleration magnitude signal with a signal anomaly.

determine the position of the anomalous point in the signal. Using interpolation, the anomalous data point shall be resolved based on the averaging of the preceding and subsequent point in the signal data, as illustrated in Figure 4.13.

The **range** and **len** methods for Python ascertain the final index to the acceleration magnitude signal using the **for** loop. With the **if** Boolean statement the anomalous aspect of the zero acceleration magnitude signal is detected. Then the average of the preceding and subsequent points of the acceleration magnitude signal replace the anomalous data point. Further analysis of the signal data reveals the associated time stamp to the anomalous acceleration signal is out of alignment with the incremental time step advance. An analogous technique applied to resolve the acceleration signal anomaly is implemented to resolve the misaligned time stamp associated to the anomalous acceleration signal.

With the syntax presented in Figure 4.13 amended to the Python software program before the programing lines for plotting defined in Requirement 4 and after the acceleration magnitude signal postprocessing aspect from Requirement 3, an improved version of the software is available. Further testing and evaluation of the refined Python software program, is applied. The anomaly in the acceleration magnitude signal is resolved as revealed in Figure 4.14. Figure 4.15 presents the preliminary structure of the ARFF file using the postprocessing of a single acceleration magnitude signal.

The preliminary version of the Python software program has been successfully applied. However, this program only processes one trial sample of the data. There are a total of 10 trials (five with deep brain

```
In [ ]:  #
         #  This aspect of the software is designed to scan for anomalous acceleration signal data that produces an
         #  anomalous zero acceleration signal.  Upon detection of anomalous zero acceleration signal, interpolation
         #  based on the averaging of the preceding and subsequent acceleration signal replaces the anomalous zero
         #  acceleration signal.  An analogous technique is applied to resolve the time stamp anomaly.
         #

         for i in range(len(accelMag)):
             if accelMag[i] == 0:
                 accelMag[i] = (accelMag[i-1]+accelMag[i+1])/2
                 time[i] = (time[i-1]+time[i+1])/2
```

Fig. 4.13. Python syntax for detecting the acceleration magnitude signal anomaly with associated time stamp anomaly and replacement through interpolation using the Jupyter Notebook.

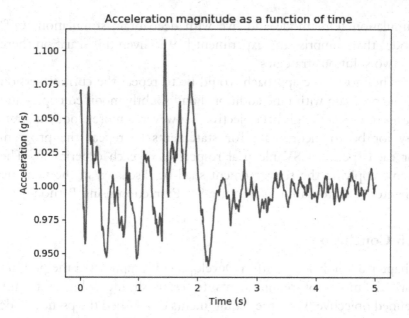

Fig. 4.14. The acceleration magnitude signal with the anomalous aspect of the signal resolved using interpolation.

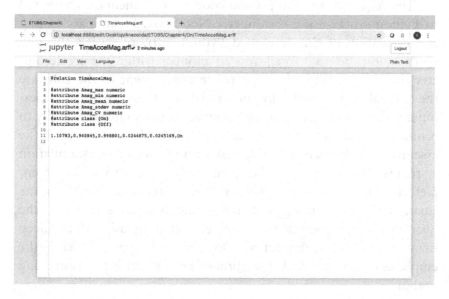

Fig. 4.15. The preliminary aspect of the ARFF file based on the consolidation of one acceleration magnitude signal.

stimulation 'On' mode and five with deep brain stimulation 'Off' mode) that comprise the experiment [19]. Given this situation there are two solution strategies.

The most basic approach would be to repeat the current version of the program with nine additional and slightly modified copies and pastes to satisfy the global objective. However, a more eloquent strategy for be to incorporate **for** statements to repeat the program for each specific CSV file trial respective of each experiment. The theme applying the **for** statement shall be discussed in the pending Chapter 5 'Automation of Feature Set Extraction using Python'.

4.5 Conclusion

Chapter 3 'Global Algorithm Development' emphasized the preliminary definition of requirements to establish the solution to the defined objective. With the requirements established the pseudo code is developed. The subsequent step for the software development process involves interleaving the requirements in conjunction with the pseudo code program.

The requirements and pseudo code are incrementally converted to Python syntax using the Jupyter Notebook. Preliminary testing and evaluation of the developed Python software reveals through visualization the need to address an anomaly within the accelerometer signal data. With the appropriate amendment to the software the anomaly is resolved using interpolation of the proximal accelerometer signal data. The Python software demonstrates the ability to produce a preliminary aspect of the ARFF file respective of the essential tremor reach and grasp task with the deep brain stimulation system set to 'On' status. The ensuing objective is to achieve complete automation of the acquired accelerometer signal data from the smartphone constituting a wearable and wireless system for the quantification of essential tremor reach and grasp task with the deep brain stimulation system set to 'On' and 'Off' status, which is the emphasis of Chapter 5 'Automation of Feature Set Extraction using Python'.

References

1. Sommerville, I. (2011). *Software Engineering*, 9th Ed., Chapter 2 "Software Processes," (Addison Wesley, New York) pp. 27–55.
2. Sommerville, I. (2011). *Software Engineering*, 9th Ed., Chapter 4 "Requirements Engineering," (Addison Wesley, New York) pp. 82–117.
3. Python [www.python.org]
4. Numpy [www.numpy.org]
5. Severance, C. (2013). *Python for Informatics: Exploring Information*, (CreateSpace).
6. LeMoyne, R., Coroian, C., Mastroianni, T., Opalinski, P., Cozza, M. and Grundfest, W. (2009). *Biomedical Engineering*, ed. Barros de Mello, C. A., Chapter 10 "The Merits of Artificial Proprioception, with Applications in Biofeedback Gait Rehabilitation Concepts and Movement Disorder Characterization," (InTech, Vienna) pp. 165–198.
7. LeMoyne, R. and Mastroianni, T. (2015). *Mobile Health Technologies, Methods and Protocols*, eds. Rasooly, A. and Herold, K. E., Chapter 23 "Use of Smartphones and Portable Media Devices for Quantifying Human Movement Characteristics of Gait, Tendon Reflex Response, and Parkinson's Disease Hand Tremor," (Springer, New York) pp. 335–358.
8. LeMoyne, R. and Mastroianni, T. (2016). *Telemedicine*, "Telemedicine Perspectives for Wearable and Wireless Applications Serving the Domain of Neurorehabilitation and Movement Disorder Treatment," (SMGroup, Dover) pp. 1–10.
9. LeMoyne, R. and Mastroianni, T. (2017). *Wireless MEMS Networks and Applications*, ed. Uttamchandani, D., Chapter 6 "Wearable and Wireless Gait Analysis Platforms: Smartphones and Portable Media Devices," (Elsevier, New York) pp. 129–152.
10. LeMoyne, R. and Mastroianni, T. (2017). *Smartphones from an Applied Research Perspective*, ed. Mohamudally, N., Chapter 1 "Smartphone and Portable Media Device: A Novel Pathway Toward the Diagnostic Characterization of Human Movement," (InTech, Rijeka) pp. 1–24.
11. LeMoyne, R. and Mastroianni, T. (2018). *Wearable and Wireless Systems for Healthcare I: Gait and Reflex Response Quantification*, (Springer, Singapore).

12. LeMoyne, R. and Mastroianni, T. (2018). *Wearable and Wireless Systems for Healthcare I: Gait and Reflex Response Quantification*, Chapter 9 "Role of Machine Learning for Gait and Reflex Response Classification," (Springer, Singapore) pp. 111–120.

13. LeMoyne, R., Mastroianni, T., Whiting, D. and Tomycz, N. (2019). *Wearable and Wireless Systems for Healthcare II: Movement Disorder Evaluation and Deep Brain Stimulation Systems*, (Springer, Singapore).

14. LeMoyne, R., Mastroianni, T., Whiting, D. and Tomycz, N. (2019). *Wearable and Wireless Systems for Healthcare II: Movement Disorder Evaluation and Deep Brain Stimulation Systems*, Chapter 8, "Role of Machine Learning for Classification of Movement Disorder and Deep Brain Stimulation Status," (Springer, Singapore) pp. 99–111.

15. LeMoyne, R. and Mastroianni, T. (2019). *Smartphones: Recent Innovations and Applications*, ed. Dabove, P., Chapter 7 "Network Centric Therapy for Wearable and Wireless Systems," (Nova Science Publishers, Hauppauge).

16. LeMoyne, R. and Mastroianni, T. (2020). *Multilayer Perceptrons: Theory and Applications*, ed. Vang-Mata, R., Chapter 2, "Machine Learning Classification for Network Centric Therapy Utilizing the Multilayer Perceptron Neural Network," (Nova Science Publishers, Hauppauge) pp. 39–76.

17. LeMoyne, R., Kerr, W., Zanjani, K. and Mastroianni, T. (2014). Implementation of an iPod wireless accelerometer application using machine learning to classify disparity of hemiplegic and healthy patellar tendon reflex pair, *J. Med. Imaging Health Inform.*, 4, pp. 21–28.

18. LeMoyne, R., Kerr, W., Mastroianni, T. and Hessel, A. (2014). Implementation of machine learning for classifying hemiplegic gait disparity through use of a force plate, *Proc. 13th International Conference on Machine Learning and Applications (ICMLA), IEEE*, pp. 379–382.

19. LeMoyne, R., Tomycz, N., Mastroianni, T., McCandless, C., Cozza, M. and Peduto, D. (2015). Implementation of a smartphone wireless accelerometer platform for establishing deep brain stimulation treatment efficacy of essential tremor with machine learning, *Proc. 37th Annual International Conference of the IEEE, Engineering in Medicine and Biology Society (EMBS)*, pp. 6772–6775.

20. LeMoyne, R., Mastroianni, T., Hessel, A. and Nishikawa, K. (2015). Implementation of machine learning for classifying prosthesis type through conventional gait analysis, *Proc. 37th Annual International Conference of the IEEE, Engineering in Medicine and Biology Society (EMBS)*, pp. 202–205.

21. LeMoyne, R. and Mastroianni, T. (2015). Machine learning classification of a hemiplegic and healthy patellar tendon reflex pair through an iPod wireless gyroscope platform, *Proc. 45th Society for Neuroscience Annual Meeting*.

22. LeMoyne, R., Kerr, W. and Mastroianni, T. (2015). Implementation of machine learning with an iPod application mounted to cane for classifying assistive device usage, *J. Med. Imaging Health Inform.*, 5, pp. 1404–1408.

23. LeMoyne, R., Mastroianni, T., Hessel, A. and Nishikawa, K. (2015). Application of a multilayer perceptron neural network for classifying software platforms of a powered prosthesis through a force plate, *Proc. 14th International Conference on Machine Learning and Applications (ICMLA), IEEE*, pp. 402–405.

24. LeMoyne, R., Mastroianni, T., Hessel, A. and Nishikawa, K. (2015). Ankle rehabilitation system with feedback from a smartphone wireless gyroscope platform and machine learning classification, *Proc. 14th International Conference on Machine Learning and Applications (ICMLA), IEEE*, pp. 406–409.

25. LeMoyne, R., Heerinckx, F., Aranca, T., De Jager, R., Zesiewicz, T. and Saal, H. J. (2016). Wearable body and wireless inertial sensors for machine learning classification of gait for people with Friedreich's ataxia, *Proc. 13th Annual International Body Sensor Networks Conference (BSN), IEEE*, pp. 147–151.

26. LeMoyne, R. and Mastroianni, T. (2016). Implementation of a smartphone as a wireless gyroscope platform for quantifying reduced arm swing in hemiplegic gait with machine learning classification by multilayer perceptron neural network, *Proc. 38th Annual International Conference of the IEEE, Engineering in Medicine and Biology Society (EMBS)*, pp. 2626–2630.

27. LeMoyne, R. and Mastroianni, T. (2016). Smartphone wireless gyroscope platform for machine learning classification of hemiplegic patellar

tendon reflex pair disparity through a multilayer perceptron neural network, *Proc. Wireless Health (WH), IEEE*, pp. 1–6.

28. LeMoyne, R. and Mastroianni, T. (2016). Implementation of a multilayer perceptron neural network for classifying a hemiplegic and healthy reflex pair using an iPod wireless gyroscope platform, *Proc. 46th Society for Neuroscience Annual Meeting.*

29. LeMoyne, R. and Mastroianni, T. (2017). Virtual Proprioception for eccentric training, *Proc. 39th Annual International Conference of the IEEE, Engineering in Medicine and Biology Society (EMBS)*, pp. 4557–4561.

30. LeMoyne, R. and Mastroianni, T. (2017). Wireless gyroscope platform enabled by a portable media device for quantifying wobble board therapy, *Proc. 39th Annual International Conference of the IEEE, Engineering in Medicine and Biology Society (EMBS)*, pp. 2662–2666.

31. LeMoyne, R. and Mastroianni, T. (2017). Implementation of a smartphone wireless gyroscope platform with machine learning for classifying disparity of a hemiplegic patellar tendon reflex pair, *J. Mech. Med. Biol.*, 17, 1750083.

32. LeMoyne, R., Mastroianni, T., Tomycz, N., Whiting, D., Oh, M., McCandless, C., Currivan, C. and Peduto, D. (2017). Implementation of a multilayer perceptron neural network for classifying deep brain stimulation in 'On' and 'Off' modes through a smartphone representing a wearable and wireless sensor application, *Proc. 47th Society for Neuroscience Annual Meeting, featured in Hot Topics (top 1% of abstracts).*

33. LeMoyne, R., Mastroianni, T., McCandless, C., Currivan, C., Whiting, D. and Tomycz, N. (2018). Implementation of a smartphone as a wearable and wireless accelerometer and gyroscope platform for ascertaining deep brain stimulation treatment efficacy of Parkinson's disease through machine learning classification, *Adv. Park. Dis.*, 7, pp. 19–30.

34. LeMoyne, R., Mastroianni, T., McCandless, C., Currivan, C., Whiting, D. and Tomycz, N. (2018). Implementation of a smartphone as a wearable and wireless inertial sensor platform for determining efficacy of deep brain stimulation for Parkinson's disease tremor through machine learning, *Proc. 48th Society for Neuroscience Annual Meeting, Nanosymposium.*

35. LeMoyne, R. and Mastroianni, T. (2018). Implementation of a smartphone as a wearable and wireless gyroscope platform for machine

learning classification of hemiplegic gait through a multilayer perceptron neural network, *Proc. 17th International Conference on Machine Learning and Applications (ICMLA), IEEE,* pp. 946–950.

36. LeMoyne, R., Mastroianni, T., Whiting, D. and Tomycz, N. (2019). *Wearable and Wireless Systems for Healthcare II: Movement Disorder Evaluation and Deep Brain Stimulation Systems,* Chapter 9, "Assessment of Machine Learning Classification Strategies for the Differentiation of Deep Brain Stimulation "On" and "Off" Status for Parkinson's Disease Using a Smartphone as a Wearable and Wireless Inertial Sensor for Quantified Feedback," (Springer, Singapore) pp. 113–126.

37. LeMoyne, R., Mastroianni, T., McCandless, C., Whiting, D. and Tomycz, N. (2019). Evaluation of machine learning algorithms for classifying deep brain stimulation respective of 'On' and 'Off' status, *Proc. 9th International IEEE Conference on Neural Engineering (NER), IEEE/EMBS,* pp. 483–488.

38. LeMoyne, R. and Mastroianni, T. (2019). Classification of software control architectures for a powered prosthesis through conventional gait analysis using machine learning applications, *J. Mech. Med. Biol.,* 19, 1950044.

39. LeMoyne, R., Mastroianni, T., Whiting, D. and Tomycz, N. (2019). Network Centric Therapy for deep brain stimulation status parametric analysis with machine learning classification, *Proc. 49th Society for Neuroscience Annual Meeting, Nanosymposium.*

40. LeMoyne, R., Mastroianni, T., Whiting, D. and Tomycz, N. (2019). Preliminary Network Centric Therapy for machine learning classification of deep brain stimulation status for the treatment of Parkinson's disease with a conformal wearable and wireless inertial sensor, *Adv. Park. Dis.,* 8, pp. 75–91.

41. Mastroianni, T. and LeMoyne, R. (2016). Application of a multilayer perceptron neural network with an iPod as a wireless gyroscope platform to classify reduced arm swing gait for people with Erb's palsy, *Proc. 46th Society for Neuroscience Annual Meeting.*

42. Hall, M., Frank, E., Holmes, G., Pfahringer, B., Reutemann, P. and Witten I. H. (2009). The WEKA data mining software: An update, *ACM SIGKDD Explor. Newsl.,* 11, pp. 10–18.

43. Witten, I. H., Frank, E. and Hall, M. A. (2011). *Data Mining: Practical Machine Learning Tools and Techniques*, 3rd Ed. (Morgan Kaufmann, Burlington).
44. WEKA [http://www.cs.waikato.ac.nz/~ml/weka/]
45. Sommerville, I. (2011). *Software Engineering*, 9th Ed., Chapter 7 "Design and Implementation," (Addison Wesley, New York) pp. 176–204.
46. Deitel, H. and Deitel, P. (2019). *Python for Programmers with Introductory AI Case Studies*, Chapter 5 "Sequences: Lists and Tuples," (Prentice Hall, New York) pp. 101–136.
47. Sommerville, I. (2011). *Software Engineering*, 9th Ed., Chapter 8 "Software Testing," (Addison Wesley, New York) pp. 205–233.

Chapter 5

Automation of Feature Set Extraction using Python

5.1 Introduction

The preliminary success of the software presented in Chapter 4 'Incremental Software Development using Python' establishes the basis for the objective of the current chapter, which is to achieve automation of the accelerometer signal data in a manner that is fully automated. This objective is facilitated by the proper organization of the respective files, retaining the accelerometer signals. The clarification of new requirements and associated pseudo code is established in alignment with the software development process, and Kaizen techniques are incorporated for improving the capability of the software [1–4].

The implementation phase of software development is reconsidered [5]. In order to achieve the new software requirements and associated pseudo code, the appropriate Python syntax is ascertained [6–10]. The demonstration of the applied syntax enables the ability to automate the essential tremor reach and grasp task using the smartphone as a wearable and wireless accelerometer system with the deep brain stimulation system set to the 'On' mode. The associated accelerometer signal acquired by the smartphone as a wearable and wireless system for the deep brain stimulation system using the 'On' mode for the essential tremor reach and grasp task is successfully illustrated [11].

The next step is to develop software using Python to fully automate the consolidation of the accelerometer signal data acquired from the smartphone as a wearable and wireless system for the deep brain stimulation system set to the 'On' and 'Off' mode regarding the reach and grasp task for the subject with essential tremor. In order to achieve this automated capability, the concept of software reuse is addressed, which facilitates the development of similar themed software applications [12, 13]. The 'Off' mode for the essential tremor reach and grasp task quantified by the smartphone as a wearable and wireless accelerometer system is successfully presented [11]. The resultant software program using Python provides automated consolidation of the accelerometer signal to a feature set amenable to the Attribute-Relation File Format (ARFF) suitable for the Waikato Environment for Knowledge Analysis (WEKA) as previously advocated and implemented [11, 14–48].

5.2 Information Organization Strategy

In tandem with the development of automation software using Python for consolidating the feature set based on the accelerometer signal data, the organization of the available and produced files should be strategically defined. The purpose is to maintain neat organization of the files in association with respective folders. This approach mitigates the possibility of developing a software automation program that requires multiple revisions in order to maintain proper organization of the available files that are utilized by the program and the output from the program.

The data source files shall be consolidated into their own respective folders. The Comma-Separated Values (CSV) files constituting experimental trials of the reach and grasp task with the deep brain stimulation system set to 'On' status shall be allocated to the **On** folder. The CSV files regarding the deep brain stimulation system set to 'Off' status for reach and grasp task shall be allocated to the **Off** folder.

Rather than commingling the experimental trial CSV files and the post-processing derived files, a delineation between these two

Fig. 5.1. The graphical representation of the recommended folder organization relative to the automation.

types of files is recommended. Therefore, the resultant graphical representations of the acceleration magnitude for the deep brain stimulation set to 'On' and 'Off' status trials shall be saved in a folder defined as **Post** (post-processing). Furthermore, the ARFF file for machine learning classification shall also be written to the **Post** folder. The organization of the recommended folders and associated automation software using Python is graphically presented in Figure 5.1.

5.3 Provisional Evolution of Requirements and Associated Pseudo Code

One particular advantage of establishing requirements that are supported by pseudo code is the evidentiary perspective respective of the thought process and progressive evolution of the software program. The coding presented in Chapter 4 'Incremental Software Development using Python' develops the foundational post-processing. With the implementation of Kaizen for continuous improvement a means for expanding the automation capabilities is sought after [1–4].

These amended requirements and associated pseudo code shall be introduced. Following this process, the appropriate Python syntax shall be presented. Preliminary demonstration pertains to solely one folder respective of the deep brain stimulation system set to 'On' status. Using the success of automation for a single directory software programming, reuse is applied to both the deep brain stimulation 'On' and 'Off' status.

The following requirements are recommended to achieve post-processing automation of the CSV acceleration signal files recorded through the application of the smartphone as a wearable and wireless inertial sensor system:

(1) Read accelerometer signal CSV files from the prescribed directory.
(2) Loop through the post-processing software presented in Chapter 4 'Incremental Software Development using Python'.
(3) Save and increment each figure file with an index.
(4) Amend the ARFF file with the newly post-processed numeric attributes.

A requirements flowchart is presented in Figure 5.2 for realizing the automation of the software.

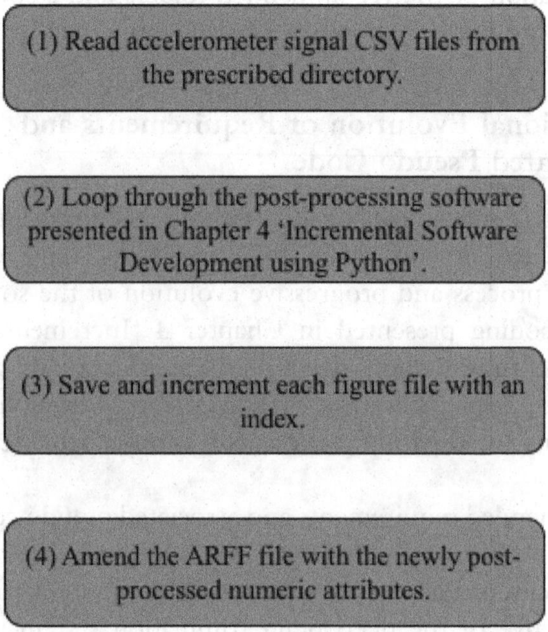

(1) Read accelerometer signal CSV files from the prescribed directory.

(2) Loop through the post-processing software presented in Chapter 4 'Incremental Software Development using Python'.

(3) Save and increment each figure file with an index.

(4) Amend the ARFF file with the newly post-processed numeric attributes.

Fig. 5.2.   Requirements flowchart for achieving the software automation.

These broader requirements can be further refined through the pseudo code subsequently presented:

(1) Ascertain the CSV files comprising the acceleration signal for the 'On' status deep brain stimulation system respective of the **On** directory into a list.

(2) With each CSV file comprising the acceleration signal ascertained, loop through the original code presented in Chapter 4 'Incremental Software Development using Python' for each file name that is presented within the list.

(3) Upon post-processing the acceleration magnitude signal save a graphical representation of the acceleration magnitude signal as a function of time that is saved with the file name incremented.

(4) For each loop cycle amend a new instance regarding the numeric attributes of the feature set to the ARFF file.

5.4 Syntax Implementation using Python

The definition of requirements and refinement of the pseudo code establish the basis for ascertaining the necessary Python syntax for implementation [5]. First, the **os** library should be imported through the **import** statement. The **os** library enables operating system specific commands. The **listdir()** method acquires the available file names to the prescribed directory defined within the parentheses of the **listdir()** method [6].

An empty list defined as **newlist** is established. The **for** statement loops through all of the files in the directory, and with the **if** statement and the **endswidth()** method the CSV files are then appended using the **append()** method to the **newlist**. The Python syntax and associated commenting are presented in Figure 5.3.

The **for** statement serves an instrumental role for achieving the automation capability. This looping statement warrants further consideration. As illustrated in Figure 5.4, the **for** statement incorporates **j** as the iteration variable, which begins at zero and increments by one for each loop through the **for** statement. The reserved keyword **in** establishes the upper bound for the definite loop **for** statement. Note the colon at the end of the **for** statement [7].

```
In [ ]:  #
         #  The file names are ascertained for the Essential tremor CSV files recording the acceleration signal recorded by
         #  the smartphone mounted about the dorsum of the hand using the Vibration application and assigned to a list
         #  consisting of the files regarding the associated /On/ directory.
         #

         import os
         items = os.listdir("./On/")

         newlist = []
         for names in items:
             if names.endswith(".csv"):
                 newlist.append(names)
```

Fig. 5.3. Python syntax for ascertaining the CSV file names and establishing a list of the CSV file names.

```
In [ ]:  #
         #  This for statement loops through the available CSV file names ascertained in the /On/ directory.
         #

         for j in range(len(newlist)):
             file='On/'+newlist[j]
```

Fig. 5.4. Python syntax for looping throughout the CSV file names ascertained in the **On** directory.

The **for** statement is known as a compound statement. The compound statement is comprised of a header and body. The terminal aspect of the head is completed with the colon. The body section of the header is relatively indented [8].

The upper bound is established the **range(len(newlist))**, which incorporates the functions **range()** and **len()**. The **len()** function returned the number of elements that comprises the list. The **range()** function establishes a list of indices spanning from zero to the length of the list less one [9].

Each element of the list comprising the file names is associated with an index. The **file** variable is a concatenation of the directory for the deep brain stimulation system 'On' status acceleration signal data and the file names correlated with the respective index. For example, with **j = 0** and **newlist[0]** = 'VibrationData 2015-01-27 at 15 49 00-email.csv', then **file** = 'On/'+newlist[j] will produce **file** = 'On/VibrationData 2015-01-27 at 15 49 00-email.csv' [10].

Furthermore, the iteration variable **j** is of integer type. In order to concatenate the iteration variable with the associated output figure file name, the iteration variable **j** should be converted from integer type to string type using the str() function. For example, when **j = 0**, the string **'Post/TimeAccelMagOn'+str(j)+'.png'** is the equivalence of **'Post/TimeAccelMagOn0.png'**. In addition, the associated file name iterative number can start with the number 1 by incrementing the str(). With **j = 0** the string **'Post/TimeAccelMagOn'+str(j+1)+'. png'** results in **'Post/TimeAccelMagOn1.png'** [10].

5.5 Rearranging Existing Python Code Outside of the Global For Statement

Further evolution of the Python software to an automated process requires identifying aspects of the software that should be rerouted outside of the global **for** statement. Basically, any aspect of the software that should be only executed once should be moved outside the **for** statement. Note the aspect of the program that writes the header section of the ARFF file should be moved outside of the **for** statement, since it only needs to be conducted once, as illustrated in Figure 5.5.

The global **for** statement is capable of post-processing all five trial samples of the CSV acceleration signal recordings. The value of automation is a significant reduction in time to complete post-processing. Furthermore, the post-processing improves the quality of the end

```
In [ ]: #
        #   The command to write the Attribute-Relation File Format (ARFF) with the fout file handle is established and
        #   assigned to the same directory associated with the directory and file name for the Essential tremor
        #   CSV file.
        #

        fout = open('On/Post/TimeAccelMag.arff', 'w')

        #
        #   The write method with the file handle object assigns the header aspect of the ARFF file. Note the definition
        #   of the @relation TimeAccelMag at the top aspect of the ARFF file. Subsequently, the @attribute defines Amag_max,
        #   Amag_min, Amag_mean, Amag_stdev, and Amag_CV for the maximum, minimum, mean, standard deviation, and coefficient
        #   of variation for the acceleration magnitude of the respective acceleration signal. Furthermore, the @attribute
        #   defines the 'On' and 'Off' classes.
        #

        fout.write('@relation TimeAccelMag\n\n')
        fout.write('@attribute Amag_max numeric\n')
        fout.write('@attribute Amag_min numeric\n')
        fout.write('@attribute Amag_mean numeric\n')
        fout.write('@attribute Amag_stdev numeric\n')
        fout.write('@attribute Amag_CV numeric\n')
        fout.write('@attribute class {On}\n')
        fout.write('@attribute class {Off}\n\n')
```

Fig. 5.5.   Python syntax identified as appropriate to be situated outside of the looping **for** statement.

product files, such as the ARFF file and figure files, since they are developed through the software commands with minimal human intervention. Figures 5.6 through 5.10 illustrate the Python software for post-processing of CSV acceleration signal data of the deep brain stimulation system 'On' status regarding an essential tremor subject conducting a reach and grasp task.

By clicking the **Run** icon on the Jupyter Notebook the software presented in Figures 5.6 through 5.10 produces as output five graphs of the acceleration magnitude signal as a function of time. The graphs are saved in the **Post** directory as Portable Network Graphics (PNG) files. In addition, Figure 5.11 displays the preliminary aspect of the ARFF file, respective of deep brain stimulation set to 'On' status. The preliminary development of the ARFF file presents the header aspect of the ARFF file and the feature set data representing the numeric attributes that correspond to the deep brain stimulation set to 'On' status for the essential tremor reach and grasp task. Figures 5.12 through 5.16 provide graphical representations of the acceleration

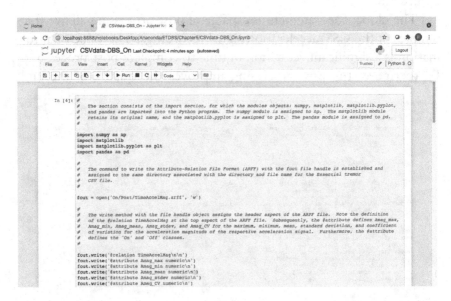

Fig. 5.6. Python program for post-processing of CSV acceleration signal data with respect to deep brain stimulation system 'On' status for an essential tremor subject conducting a reach and grasp task (page 1).

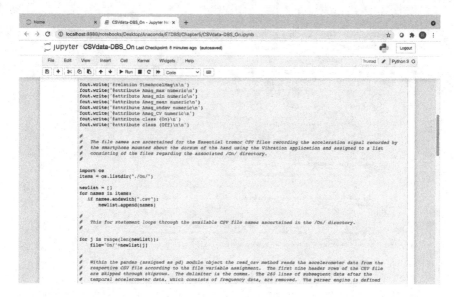

Fig. 5.7. Python program for post-processing of CSV acceleration signal data with respect to deep brain stimulation system 'On' status for an essential tremor subject conducting a reach and grasp task (page 2).

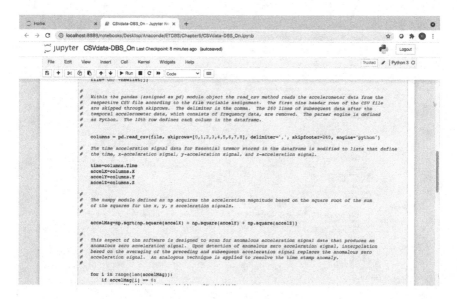

Fig. 5.8. Python program for post-processing of CSV acceleration signal data with respect to deep brain stimulation system 'On' status for an essential tremor subject conducting a reach and grasp task (page 3).

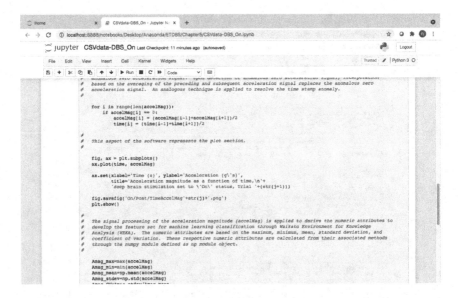

Fig. 5.9.   Python program for post-processing of CSV acceleration signal data with respect to deep brain stimulation system 'On' status for an essential tremor subject conducting a reach and grasp task (page 4).

Fig. 5.10.   Python program for post-processing of CSV acceleration signal data with respect to deep brain stimulation system 'On' status for an essential tremor subject conducting a reach and grasp task (page 5).

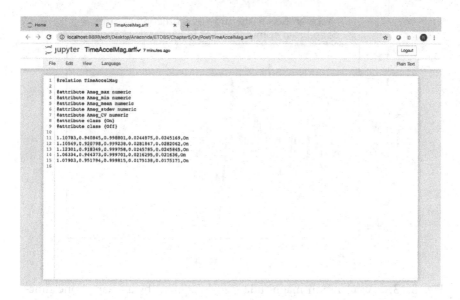

Fig. 5.11. The preliminary development of the ARFF file, consisting of a header section and the feature set numeric attributes for the essential tremor subject conducting a reach and grasp task with the deep brain stimulation system set to 'On' status.

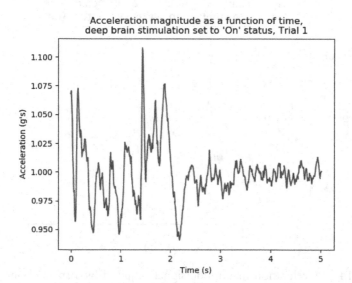

Fig. 5.12. Acceleration magnitude signal acquired by a smartphone functioning as a wearable and wireless inertial sensor system for quantifying essential tremor characteristics of a reach and grasp task with deep brain stimulation set to 'On' status, Trial 1.

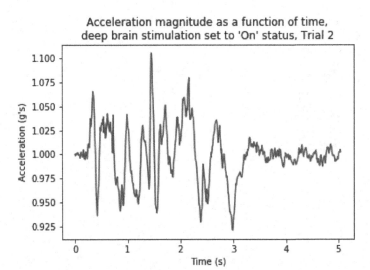

Fig. 5.13. Acceleration magnitude signal acquired by a smartphone functioning as a wearable and wireless inertial sensor system for quantifying essential tremor characteristics of a reach and grasp task with deep brain stimulation set to 'On' status, Trial 2.

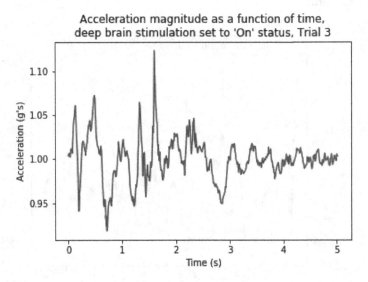

Fig. 5.14. Acceleration magnitude signal acquired by a smartphone functioning as a wearable and wireless inertial sensor system for quantifying essential tremor characteristics of a reach and grasp task with deep brain stimulation set to 'On' status, Trial 3.

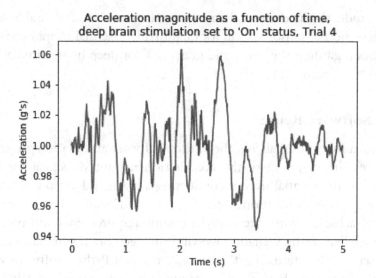

Fig. 5.15. Acceleration magnitude signal acquired by a smartphone functioning as a wearable and wireless inertial sensor system for quantifying essential tremor characteristics of a reach and grasp task with deep brain stimulation set to 'On' status, Trial 4.

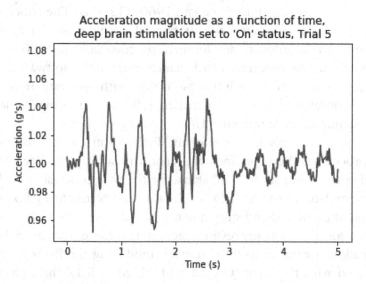

Fig. 5.16. Acceleration magnitude signal acquired by a smartphone functioning as a wearable and wireless inertial sensor system for quantifying essential tremor characteristics of a reach and grasp task with deep brain stimulation set to 'On' status, Trial 5.

magnitude signal derived from the smartphone as a wearable and wireless inertial sensor system for quantifying essential tremor characteristics regarding the reach and grasp task for deep brain stimulation set to 'On' status [11].

5.6 Software Reuse

The next aspect of realizing the Python software automation program requires the graphing of the acceleration magnitude signal for the subject with essential tremor conducting a reach and grasp task while the deep brain stimulation system is set to 'Off' status. This endeavor can be achieved with effectively the same requirements and pseudo code applied to the scenario involving the deep brain stimulation system set to 'On' status. Furthermore, the actual Python software syntax presented in Figures 5.6 through 5.10 is readily capable of resolving the post-processing for the deep brain stimulation system set to 'Off' status with minimal modifications. This observation introduces the perspective of software reuse.

Software reuse was proposed as an evolution to the software development process during the late 1960s [12, 13]. The concept of software reuse incorporates the strategy of applying previously used software into the software development process. Since the 2000s software reuse has become a standard characteristic of the software development process. Some utilities associated with software reuse are reduced development costs, increased reliability, improved quality, and streamlined development [13].

In order to apply the reuse of the Python software for successful post-processing the experimental scenario regarding the deep brain stimulation system set to 'On' status for the post-processing of deep brain stimulation system set to 'Off' status, the pertinent Python syntax should be copied and subsequently pasted. The only major modification for the post-processing section regarding the deep brain stimulation system set to 'Off' status is modifying the Python syntax associated with the term 'On' to 'Off'. Figures 5.17 through 5.24 present the Python software for post-processing of CSV acceleration signal data of the deep brain stimulation system 'On' status and 'Off'

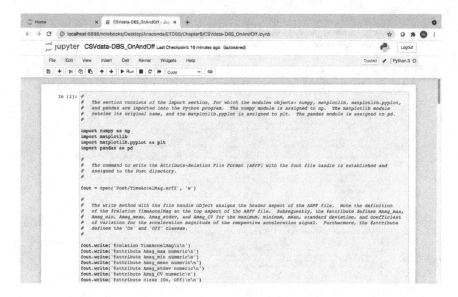

Fig. 5.17. Python program for post-processing of CSV acceleration signal data with respect to deep brain stimulation system 'On' and 'Off' status for an essential tremor subject conducting a reach and grasp task (page 1).

Fig. 5.18. Python program for post-processing of CSV acceleration signal data with respect to deep brain stimulation system 'On' and 'Off' status for an essential tremor subject conducting a reach and grasp task (page 2).

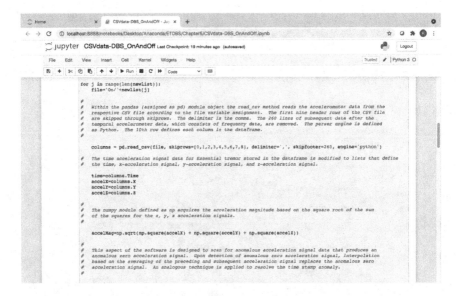

Fig. 5.19. Python program for post-processing of CSV acceleration signal data with respect to deep brain stimulation system 'On' and 'Off' status for an essential tremor subject conducting a reach and grasp task (page 3).

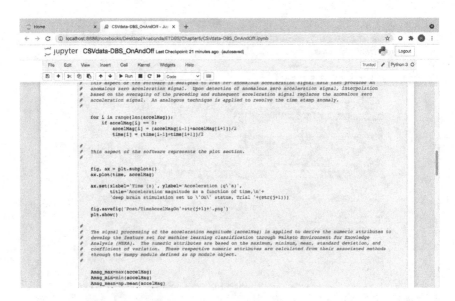

Fig. 5.20. Python program for post-processing of CSV acceleration signal data with respect to deep brain stimulation system 'On' and 'Off' status for an essential tremor subject conducting a reach and grasp task (page 4).

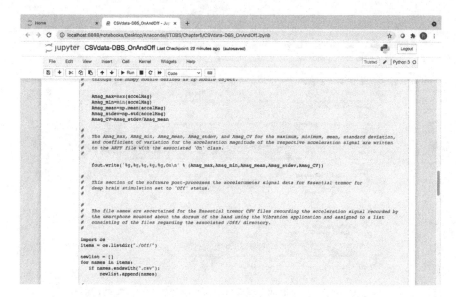

Fig. 5.21. Python program for post-processing of CSV acceleration signal data with respect to deep brain stimulation system 'On' and 'Off' status for an essential tremor subject conducting a reach and grasp task (page 5).

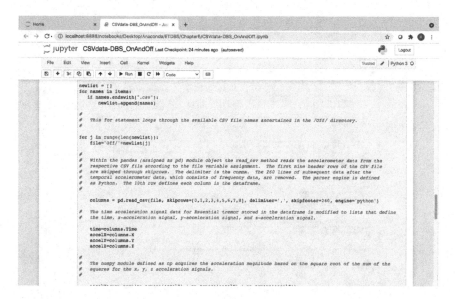

Fig. 5.22. Python program for post-processing of CSV acceleration signal data with respect to deep brain stimulation system 'On' and 'Off' status for an essential tremor subject conducting a reach and grasp task (page 6).

Fig. 5.23. Python program for post-processing of CSV acceleration signal data with respect to deep brain stimulation system 'On' and 'Off' status for an essential tremor subject conducting a reach and grasp task (page 7).

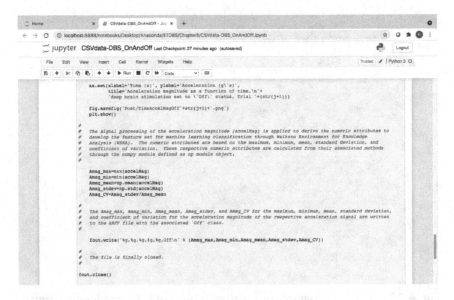

Fig. 5.24. Python program for post-processing of CSV acceleration signal data with respect to deep brain stimulation system 'On' and 'Off' status for an essential tremor subject conducting a reach and grasp task (page 8).

status for a subject with essential tremor while conducting a reach and grasp task.

By clicking the **Run** icon on the Jupyter Notebook, the software presented in Figures 5.17 through 5.24 develops 10 graphs for the acceleration magnitude signal as a function of time (five for deep brain stimulation 'On' status and five for deep brain stimulation 'Off' status) and one ARFF file. These 10 graphs are saved in the **Post** directory as PNG files. Figure 5.25 represents the complete feature set for the ARFF file with regard to deep brain stimulation set to 'On' and 'Off' status for the essential tremor reach and grasp task. Figures 5.26 through 5.30 provide graphical demonstrations of the acceleration magnitude signal using from the smartphone as a wearable and wireless inertial sensor system for quantifying essential tremor characteristics regarding the reach and grasp task for deep brain stimulation set to 'Off' status [11].

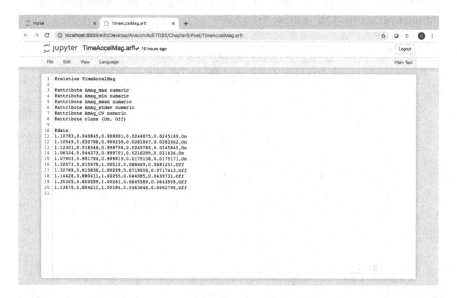

Fig. 5.25.   The fully developed ARFF file, consisting of a header section and the feature set numeric attributes for the essential tremor subject conducting a reach and grasp task with the deep brain stimulation system set to 'On' status and 'Off' status.

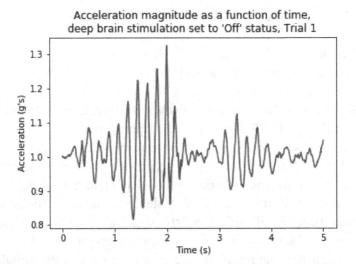

Fig. 5.26. Acceleration magnitude signal acquired by a smartphone functioning as a wearable and wireless inertial sensor system for quantifying essential tremor characteristics of a reach and grasp task with deep brain stimulation set to 'Off' status, Trial 1.

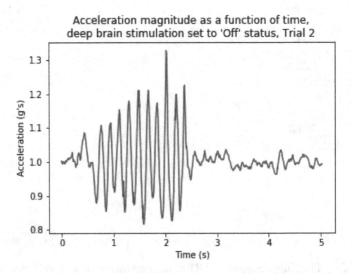

Fig. 5.27. Acceleration magnitude signal acquired by a smartphone functioning as a wearable and wireless inertial sensor system for quantifying essential tremor characteristics of a reach and grasp task with deep brain stimulation set to 'Off' status, Trial 2.

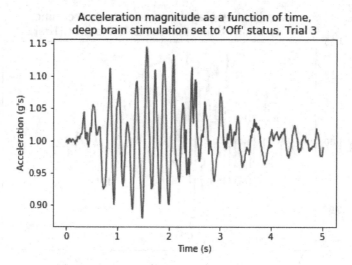

Fig. 5.28.   Acceleration magnitude signal acquired by a smartphone functioning as a wearable and wireless inertial sensor system for quantifying essential tremor characteristics of a reach and grasp task with deep brain stimulation set to 'Off' status, Trial 3.

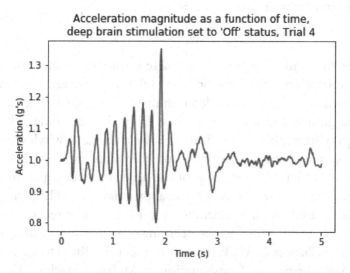

Fig. 5.29.   Acceleration magnitude signal acquired by a smartphone functioning as a wearable and wireless inertial sensor system for quantifying essential tremor characteristics of a reach and grasp task with deep brain stimulation set to 'Off' status, Trial 4.

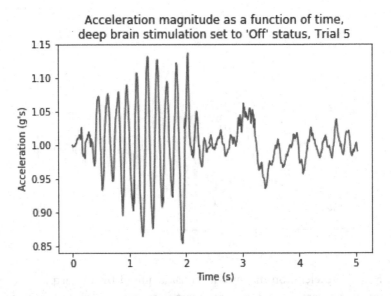

Fig. 5.30. Acceleration magnitude signal acquired by a smartphone functioning as a wearable and wireless inertial sensor system for quantifying essential tremor characteristics of a reach and grasp task with deep brain stimulation set to 'Off' status, Trial 5.

The ARFF file comprises a complete feature set of numeric attributes to characterize the deep brain stimulation system set to 'On' and 'Off' status based on the acceleration magnitude signal. The acceleration magnitude signal data is derived from the recordings obtained through a smartphone constituting a wearable and wireless inertial sensor system. The achievement of this software program using Python enables post-processing of the accelerometer signal to a feature set amenable to the ARFF file appropriate for WEKA as previously advocated and implemented [11, 14–51]. The resultant ARFF file is now ready for machine learning classification, which is the theme for Chapter 6 'Waikato Environment for Knowledge Analysis (WEKA) a Perspective Consideration of Multiple Machine Learning Classification Algorithms and Applications'.

5.7 Conclusion

Chapter 4 'Incremental Software Development using Python' develops the foundation for the fully automated software using Python to consolidate the accelerometer signal data from a smartphone as a wearable and wireless system for the essential tremor reach and grasp task with respect to deep brain stimulation set to 'On' and 'Off' to an ARFF file. Preliminarily, the accelerometer signal data files and the generated files are organized into appropriate folders. Requirements are reviewed for further amendment in conjunction with associated pseudo code for achieving the objective of automated post-processing. Subsequently, the appropriate Python syntax is applied with existing Python code and rearranged with respect to the established loop for achieving automated post-processing. Execution of the developed Python software program presents the visualization of the accelerometer signal data regarding the deep brain stimulation set to 'On' and 'Off' status for the essential tremor reach and grasp task with the development of the ARFF file for machine learning classification through the WEKA.

In order to conduct machine learning classification through WEKA, a general perspective of the operating procedure is imperative. In addition, a foundation for the principles of the selected machine learning algorithms is recommended. Chapter 6 'Waikato Environment for Knowledge Analysis (WEKA) a Perspective Consideration of Multiple Machine Learning Classification Algorithms and Applications' addresses the domain of the general operation of the selected machine learning algorithms through WEKA and their conceptual basis for distinguishing classes of the respective feature set.

References

1. Sommerville, I. (2011). *Software Engineering*, 9th Ed., Chapter 2 "Software Processes," (Addison Wesley, New York) pp. 27–55.
2. Sommerville, I. (2011). *Software Engineering*, 9th Ed., Chapter 4 "Requirements Engineering," (Addison Wesley, New York) pp. 82–117.

3. Kaizen [www.kaizen.com]

4. Kaizen Glossary [www.kaizen.com/learn-kaizen/glossary.html]

5. Sommerville, I. (2011). *Software Engineering*, 9th Ed., Chapter 7 "Design and Implementation," (Addison Wesley, New York) pp. 176–204.

6. Python Library [docs.python.org/3/library]

7. Severance, C. (2013). *Python for Informatics: Exploring Information*, Chapter 5 "Iteration," (CreateSpace) pp. 57–66.

8. Severance, C. (2013). *Python for Informatics: Exploring Information*, Chapter 3 "Conditional Execution," (CreateSpace) pp. 31–42.

9. Severance, C. (2013). *Python for Informatics: Exploring Information*, Chapter 8 "Lists," (CreateSpace) pp. 91–106.

10. Severance, C. (2013). *Python for Informatics: Exploring Information*, Chapter 2 "Variables, Expressions and Statements," (CreateSpace) pp. 19–30.

11. LeMoyne, R., Tomycz, N., Mastroianni, T., McCandless, C., Cozza, M. and Peduto, D. (2015). Implementation of a smartphone wireless accelerometer platform for establishing deep brain stimulation treatment efficacy of essential tremor with machine learning, *Proc. 37th Annual International Conference of the IEEE, Engineering in Medicine and Biology Society (EMBS)*, pp. 6772–6775.

12. McIlroy, M. D. (1968). Mass-produced software components, *Proc. NATO Software Engineering Conference*, pp. 138–156.

13. Sommerville, I. (2011). *Software Engineering*, 9th Ed., Chapter 16 "Software Reuse," (Addison Wesley, New York) pp. 425–451.

14. LeMoyne, R., Coroian, C., Mastroianni, T., Opalinski, P., Cozza, M. and Grundfest W. (2009). *Biomedical Engineering*, ed. Barros de Mello, C. A., Chapter 10 "The Merits of Artificial Proprioception, with Applications in Biofeedback Gait Rehabilitation Concepts and Movement Disorder Characterization," (InTech, Vienna), pp. 165–198.

15. LeMoyne, R. and Mastroianni, T. (2015). *Mobile Health Technologies, Methods and Protocols*, eds. Rasooly, A. and Herold, K. E., Chapter 23 "Use of Smartphones and Portable Media Devices for Quantifying Human Movement Characteristics of Gait, Tendon Reflex Response, and Parkinson's Disease Hand Tremor," (Springer, New York) pp. 335–358.

16. LeMoyne, R. and Mastroianni, T. (2016). *Telemedicine*, "Telemedicine Perspectives for Wearable and Wireless Applications Serving the Domain of Neurorehabilitation and Movement Disorder Treatment," (SMGroup, Dover) pp. 1–10.

17. LeMoyne, R. and Mastroianni, T. (2017). *Wireless MEMS Networks and Applications*, ed. Uttamchandani, D., Chapter 6 "Wearable and Wireless Gait Analysis Platforms: Smartphones and Portable Media Devices," (Elsevier, New York) pp. 129–152.

18. LeMoyne, R. and Mastroianni, T. (2017). *Smartphones from an Applied Research Perspective*, ed. Mohamudally, N., Chapter 1 "Smartphone and Portable Media Device: A Novel Pathway Toward the Diagnostic Characterization of Human Movement," (InTech, Rijeka) pp. 1–24.

19. LeMoyne, R. and Mastroianni, T. (2018). *Wearable and Wireless Systems for Healthcare I: Gait and Reflex Response Quantification*, (Springer, Singapore).

20. LeMoyne, R. and Mastroianni, T. (2018). *Wearable and Wireless Systems for Healthcare I: Gait and Reflex Response Quantification*, Chapter 9 "Role of Machine Learning for Gait and Reflex Response Classification," (Springer, Singapore) pp. 111–120.

21. LeMoyne, R., Mastroianni, T., Whiting, D. and Tomycz, N. (2019). *Wearable and Wireless Systems for Healthcare II: Movement Disorder Evaluation and Deep Brain Stimulation Systems*, (Springer, Singapore).

22. LeMoyne, R., Mastroianni, T., Whiting, D. and Tomycz, N. (2019). *Wearable and Wireless Systems for Healthcare II: Movement Disorder Evaluation and Deep Brain Stimulation Systems*, Chapter 8 "Role of Machine Learning for Classification of Movement Disorder and Deep Brain Stimulation Status," (Springer, Singapore) pp. 99–111.

23. LeMoyne, R. and Mastroianni, T. (2019). *Smartphones: Recent Innovations and Applications*, ed. Dabove, P., Chapter 7 "Network Centric Therapy for Wearable and Wireless Systems," (Nova Science Publishers, Hauppauge).

24. LeMoyne, R. and Mastroianni, T. (2020). *Multilayer Perceptrons: Theory and Applications*, ed. Vang-Mata, R., Chapter 2 "Machine Learning Classification for Network Centric Therapy Utilizing the Multilayer Perceptron Neural Network," (Nova Science Publishers, Hauppauge) pp. 39–76.

25. LeMoyne, R., Kerr, W., Zanjani, K. and Mastroianni, T. (2014). Implementation of an iPod wireless accelerometer application using machine learning to classify disparity of hemiplegic and healthy patellar tendon reflex pair, *J. Med. Imaging Health Inform.*, 4, pp. 21–28.

26. LeMoyne, R., Kerr, W., Mastroianni, T. and Hessel, A. (2014). Implementation of machine learning for classifying hemiplegic gait disparity through use of a force plate, *Proc. 13th International Conference on Machine Learning and Applications (ICMLA)*, IEEE, pp. 379–382.

27. LeMoyne, R., Mastroianni, T., Hessel, A. and Nishikawa, K. (2015). Implementation of machine learning for classifying prosthesis type through conventional gait analysis, *Proc. 37th Annual International Conference of the IEEE, Engineering in Medicine and Biology Society (EMBS)*, pp. 202–205.

28. LeMoyne, R. and Mastroianni, T. (2015). Machine learning classification of a hemiplegic and healthy patellar tendon reflex pair through an iPod wireless gyroscope platform, *Proc. 45th Society for Neuroscience Annual Meeting*.

29. LeMoyne, R., Kerr, W. and Mastroianni, T. (2015). Implementation of machine learning with an iPod application mounted to cane for classifying assistive device usage, *J. Med. Imaging Health Inform.*, 5, pp. 1404–1408.

30. LeMoyne, R., Mastroianni, T., Hessel, A. and Nishikawa, K. (2015). Application of a multilayer perceptron neural network for classifying software platforms of a powered prosthesis through a force plate, *Proc. 14th International Conference on Machine Learning and Applications (ICMLA)*, IEEE, pp. 402–405.

31. LeMoyne, R., Mastroianni, T., Hessel, A. and Nishikawa, K. (2015). Ankle rehabilitation system with feedback from a smartphone wireless gyroscope platform and machine learning classification, *Proc. 14th International Conference on Machine Learning and Applications (ICMLA)*, IEEE, pp. 406–409.

32. LeMoyne, R., Heerinckx, F., Aranca, T., De Jager, R., Zesiewicz, T. and Saal, H. J. (2016). Wearable body and wireless inertial sensors for machine learning classification of gait for people with Friedreich's ataxia, *Proc. 13th Annual International Body Sensor Networks Conference (BSN)*, IEEE, pp. 147–151.

33. LeMoyne, R. and Mastroianni, T. (2016). Implementation of a smart-phone as a wireless gyroscope platform for quantifying reduced arm swing in hemiplegic gait with machine learning classification by multi-layer perceptron neural network, *Proc. 38th Annual International Conference of the IEEE, Engineering in Medicine and Biology Society (EMBS)*, pp. 2626–2630.

34. LeMoyne, R. and Mastroianni, T. (2016). Smartphone wireless gyro-scope platform for machine learning classification of hemiplegic patellar tendon reflex pair disparity through a multilayer perceptron neural net-work, *Proc. Wireless Health (WH), IEEE*, pp. 1–6.

35. LeMoyne, R. and Mastroianni, T. (2016). Implementation of a multi-layer perceptron neural network for classifying a hemiplegic and healthy reflex pair using an iPod wireless gyroscope platform, *Proc. 46th Society for Neuroscience Annual Meeting.*

36. LeMoyne, R. and Mastroianni, T. (2017). Virtual Proprioception for eccentric training, *Proc. 39th Annual International Conference of the IEEE, Engineering in Medicine and Biology Society (EMBS)*, pp. 4557–4561.

37. LeMoyne, R. and Mastroianni, T. (2017). Wireless gyroscope platform enabled by a portable media device for quantifying wobble board ther-apy, *Proc. 39th Annual International Conference of the IEEE, Engineering in Medicine and Biology Society (EMBS)*, pp. 2662–2666.

38. LeMoyne, R. and Mastroianni, T. (2017). Implementation of a smart-phone wireless gyroscope platform with machine learning for classifying disparity of a hemiplegic patellar tendon reflex pair, *J. Mech. Med. Biol.*, 17, 1750083.

39. LeMoyne, R., Mastroianni, T., Tomycz, N., Whiting, D., Oh, M., McCandless, C., Currivan, C. and Peduto, D. (2017). Implementation of a multilayer perceptron neural network for classifying deep brain stimulation in 'On' and 'Off' modes through a smartphone representing a wearable and wireless sensor application, *Proc. 47th Society for Neuroscience Annual Meeting, Featured in Hot Topics (Top 1% of Abstracts).*

40. LeMoyne, R., Mastroianni, T., McCandless, C., Currivan, C., Whiting, D. and Tomycz, N. (2018). Implementation of a smartphone as a wear-able and wireless accelerometer and gyroscope platform for ascertaining

deep brain stimulation treatment efficacy of Parkinson's disease through machine learning classification, *Adv. Park. Dis.*, 7, pp. 19–30.

41. LeMoyne, R., Mastroianni, T., McCandless, C., Currivan, C., Whiting, D. and Tomycz, N. (2018). Implementation of a smartphone as a wearable and wireless inertial sensor platform for determining efficacy of deep brain stimulation for Parkinson's disease tremor through machine learning, *Proc. 48th Society for Neuroscience Annual Meeting, Nanosymposium.*

42. LeMoyne, R. and Mastroianni, T. (2018). Implementation of a smartphone as a wearable and wireless gyroscope platform for machine learning classification of hemiplegic gait through a multilayer perceptron neural network, *Proc. 17th International Conference on Machine Learning and Applications (ICMLA), IEEE*, pp. 946–950.

43. LeMoyne, R., Mastroianni, T., Whiting, D. and Tomycz, N. (2019). *Wearable and Wireless Systems for Healthcare II: Movement Disorder Evaluation and Deep Brain Stimulation Systems,* Chapter 9 "Assessment of Machine Learning Classification Strategies for the Differentiation of Deep Brain Stimulation "On" and "Off" Status for Parkinson's Disease Using a Smartphone as a Wearable and Wireless Inertial Sensor for Quantified Feedback," (Springer, Singapore) pp. 113–126.

44. LeMoyne, R., Mastroianni, T., McCandless, C., Whiting, D. and Tomycz, N. (2019). Evaluation of machine learning algorithms for classifying deep brain stimulation respective of 'On' and 'Off' status, *Proc. 9th International IEEE Conference on Neural Engineering (NER), IEEE/EMBS*, pp. 483–488.

45. LeMoyne, R. and Mastroianni, T. (2019). Classification of software control architectures for a powered prosthesis through conventional gait analysis using machine learning applications, *J. Mech. Med. Biol.*, 19, 1950044.

46. LeMoyne, R., Mastroianni, T., Whiting, D. and Tomycz, N. (2019). Network Centric Therapy for deep brain stimulation status parametric analysis with machine learning classification, *Proc. 49th Society for Neuroscience Annual Meeting, Nanosymposium.*

47. LeMoyne, R., Mastroianni, T., Whiting, D. and Tomycz, N. (2019). Preliminary Network Centric Therapy for machine learning classification of deep brain stimulation status for the treatment of Parkinson's disease

with a conformal wearable and wireless inertial sensor, *Adv. Park. Dis.*, 8, pp. 75–91.

48. Mastroianni, T. and LeMoyne, R. (2016). Application of a multilayer perceptron neural network with an iPod as a wireless gyroscope platform to classify reduced arm swing gait for people with Erb's palsy, *Proc. 46th Society for Neuroscience Annual Meeting*.

49. Hall, M., Frank, E., Holmes, G., Pfahringer, B., Reutemann, P. and Witten I. H. (2009). The WEKA data mining software: An update, *ACM SIGKDD Explor. Newsl.*, 11, pp. 10–18.

50. Witten, I. H., Frank, E. and Hall, M. A. (2011). *Data Mining: Practical Machine Learning Tools and Techniques*, 3rd Ed. (Morgan Kaufmann Publishers, Burlington).

51. WEKA [www.cs.waikato.ac.nz/~ml/weka]

Chapter 6

Waikato Environment for Knowledge Analysis (WEKA) a Perspective Consideration of Multiple Machine Learning Classification Algorithms and Applications

6.1 Introduction

Chapter 5 'Automation of Feature Set Extraction using Python' demonstrated the basis for extracting accelerometer signal data from a series of CSV files acquired through a smartphone functioning as a wearable and wireless accelerometer system. The experiment involved an essential tremor subject performing a reach and grasp task with respect to deep brain stimulation set to 'On' and 'Off' status [1]. Python was implemented to automate the consolidation of the acceleration magnitude signal data into numeric attributes to compose the Attribute-Relation File Format (ARFF). These achievements are in alignment with previously advocated and implemented strategies involving machine learning to distinguish various health status scenarios based on the quantified signal data acquired by wearable and wireless inertial sensor systems [1–36]. The machine learning classification accomplishments are attained through the Waikato Environment for Knowledge Analysis (WEKA), which is a highly robust machine learning algorithm platform [37–39]. As demonstrated by Figure 5.25 of Chapter 5 'Automation of Feature Set Extraction using Python' the

ARFF file has been successfully developed through automation using Python software. The next step is the implementation of WEKA to achieve machine learning classification accuracy to distinguish between deep brain stimulation set to 'On' and 'Off' status. The object of the current Chapter is to present an operational perspective of WEKA for its pending usage for machine learning classification.

6.2 Operational Perspective of WEKA

6.2.1 *Opening WEKA*

WEKA can be commenced through clicking the WEKA icon, which is represented by the weka bird of New Zealand where the University of Waikato resides. Upon beginning WEKA, the Weka graphical user interface (GUI) Chooser is opened. The Weka Explorer is available through clicking the **Explorer** button as shown in Figure 6.1 [37–39].

Fig. 6.1. The Weka GUI Chooser with the **Explorer** button [37–39].

6.2.2 *Weka Explorer Preprocess Panel*

The Weka Explorer consists of multiple panels for conducting the machine learning classification process. The first aspect of the Weka Explorer is the **Preprocess** panel, for which there is an **Open file** aspect of the panel with the **Open** button for uploading an ARFF file, as represented in Figures 6.2 and 6.3 [37–39].

Another aspect of the Weka Explorer **Preprocess** panel is the **Current relation** section. This section represents the **Relation**, such as TimeAccelMag, the number of **Instances**, which regarding this machine learning classification scenario are the total number of ten

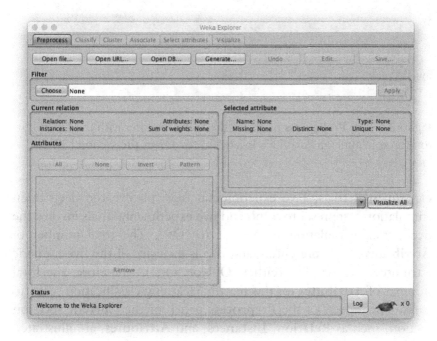

Fig. 6.2.   The **Preprocess** panel for the Weka Explorer with the **Open file** button [37–39].

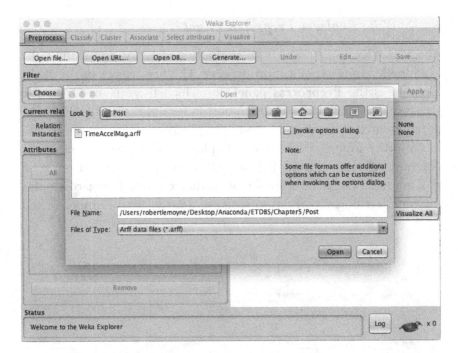

Fig. 6.3.   The **Preprocess** panel for the Weka Explorer with the **Open** button for uploading an ARFF file located in the **Open file** section [37–39].

experimental trials. Five experimental trials involve the deep brain stimulation system set to 'On', and five experimental trials involve the deep brain stimulation system set to 'Off'. The total number of **Attributes** is also presented, and this is inclusive of the five numeric attributes and the class (either 'On' or 'Off'). Therefore, the total number of **Attributes** for this machine learning classification scenario is six. The aspects of the **Preprocess** panel for the **Current relation** section, such as **Relation, Instances,** and **Attributes,** are illustrated in Figure 6.4 [37–39].

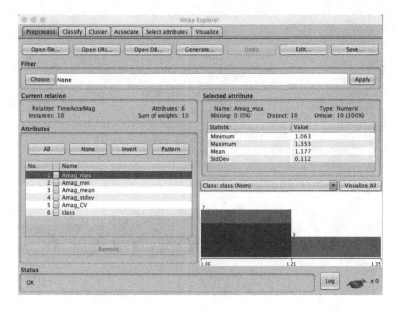

Fig. 6.4. The **Current relation** section of the **Preprocess** panel featuring the **Relation, Instances,** and **Attributes** [37–39].

Another significant section of the Weka Explorer **Preprocess** panel represents the actual attributes through the **Attributes** section, which includes both the five numeric attributes and class for this machine learning classification scenario. By cycling through the attributes, note that the graphic visualization to the right side of the panel adapts to the selected attribute. These attributes can be removed through checking the selected attribute and selecting the **Remove** button, which can be repealed through the **Undo** button. The **Attributes** section, the associated buttons, and attribute check boxes for modifying the contents of the machine learning classification feature set are presented in Figure 6.5 [37–39].

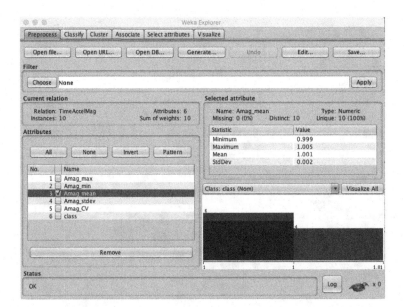

Fig. 6.5. The **Attributes** section of the Weka Explorer **Preprocess** panel with attribute check boxes (Amag_mean selected), **Remove** button, and **Undo** button for modifying the respective feature set [37–39].

The Weka Explorer **Preprocess** panel also features the capacity to edit the ARFF file at the discretion of the machine learning classification team. By selecting **Edit** button the ARFF file is presented, for which each respective cell containing feature set attributes can be modified. Amendments to the ARFF file can be preserved through the **Save** button. Figure 6.6 illustrates the editing capability for the ARFF file through the Weka Explorer **Preprocess** panel [37–39].

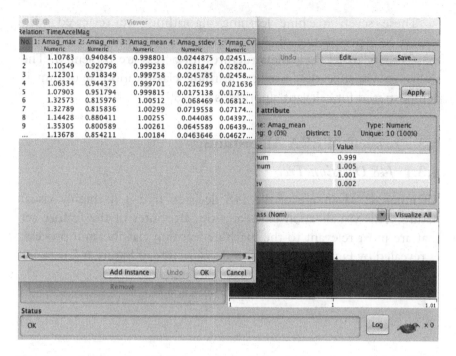

Fig. 6.6. Editing the ARFF through the **Edit** and **Save** button of the Weka Explorer **Preprocess** panel [37–39].

6.2.3 *Weka Explorer Classify Panel*

Another panel available through the Weka Explorer is the **Classify** panel. The **Classify** panel enables the selection of the machine learning classification algorithm and the methodological implementation of the machine learning classification [37–39]. Emphasis is placed on seven machine learning algorithms:

(1) J48 decision tree
(2) K-nearest neighbors
(3) Logistic regression
(4) Naïve Bayes
(5) Support vector machine
(6) Random forest
(7) Multilayer perceptron neural network

These seven machine learning algorithms are reviewed with respect to a perspective of their operational principles. From within the **Classify** panel their file structures for access are presented. The ability to visualize the machine learning classification algorithm is demonstrated for relevant algorithms [37–39].

6.3 Prevalent WEKA Algorithms

6.3.1 *J48 Decision Tree*

An inherent advantage of the J48 decision tree is its highly visual nature. This visualization elucidates the attributes of the feature set that are most relevant to the machine learning classification process, as revealed by Figure 6.7. The J48 decision tree of Figure 6.7 pertains

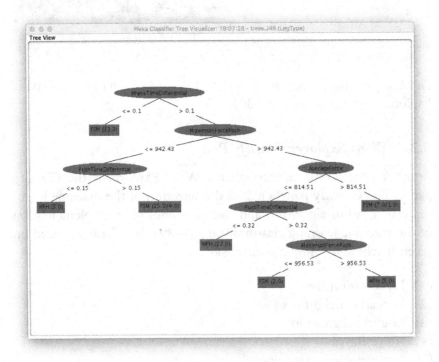

Fig. 6.7.   A J48 decision tree for differentiating between two disparate software control architectures for a transtibial-powered prosthesis [33].

to the machine learning classification to differentiate between two disparate software control architectures for a transtibial-powered prosthesis [33].

This machine learning classification scenario pertaining to the J48 decision tree for distinguishing between two software control architectures for regulating a transtibial-powered prosthesis only incorporates four of the five available numeric attributes for the feature set. The implication of this visualized J48 decision tree is that one of the five numeric attributes is not necessarily imperative for achieving the machine learning classification accuracy. Therefore, the consolidation of the data to a feature set can be reduced from five numeric attributes to four numeric attributes, which may alleviate computational processing requirements [33].

The J48 decision tree utilized by WEKA is derived from the C4-5 machine learning algorithm [37–39]. The C4-5 machine learning algorithm is an evolution of ID3, which have been both developed by Quinlan [40–42]. The C4-5 algorithm is written in C, and given the robust application of the C4-5, it has been rated as a preferred machine learning algorithm [43]. The foundation to the both the C4-5 and ID3 algorithms is the concept of information theory [37–39, 41, 42].

Information theory applies the measurement of information known as the information gain preceding and subsequent to the separation by a decision tree branch. The decision tree branching that achieves the highest information gain is deemed the most appropriate. The information gain is quantified through ascertaining the entropy, which pertains to the domain of information theory [44].

In summary, the J48 decision tree utilized through WEKA incorporates a top-down scheme using a recursive divide and conquer approach. The objective is to maximize the information gain. Information gain is acquired through the computation of the Shannon entropy (also known in information theory as entropy), which is defined in units of bits [37–39, 44].

The implementation of the J48 decision tree is achieved through the **Classify** panel of the Weka Explorer. Within the **Classifier** section

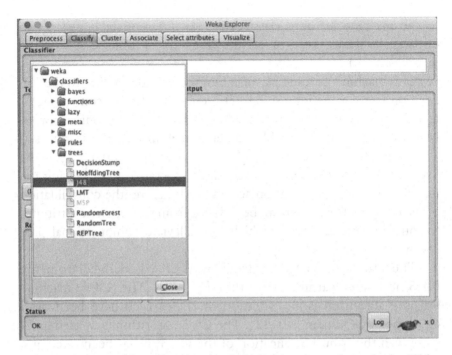

Fig. 6.8. Process for selecting the J48 decision tree through the Weka Explorer [37–39].

of the respective panel, the selection of the **Choose** icon presents an assortment of classifiers. Within these classifiers is the **trees** file structure and **J48** that represents the J48 decision tree. A representative screen capture for selecting the J48 decision tree is presented in Figure 6.8 [37–39].

With the appropriate ARFF file the uploaded J48 decision tree can provide a classification accuracy and associated output through pressing the **Start** icon below the **Test options** section. The **Result list** section provides access to the respective machine learning classification scenario, and the resultant decision tree can be produced by right-clicking the desired scenario from the **Result list** section and selecting the **Visualize tree** option. The process for obtaining the visualized J48 decision tree is provided in Figure 6.9 [37–39].

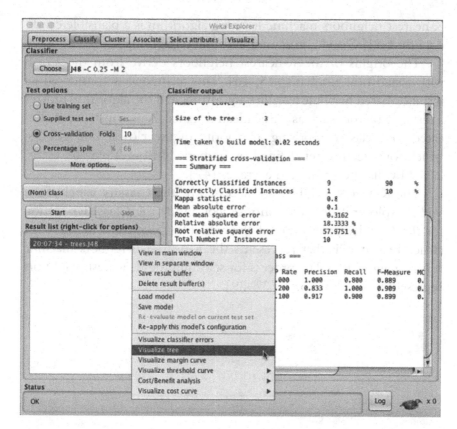

Fig. 6.9. Process for developing the visualization of the J48 decision tree [37–39].

6.3.2 *K-Nearest Neighbors*

K-nearest neighbors offers a robust machine learning classification scheme. With respect to the consideration of multiple machine learning classification algorithms for attaining classification accuracy to distinguish between two disparate software control architectures for a transtibial-powered prosthesis, the K-nearest neighbors algorithm demonstrated the greatest classification accuracy [33]. Another advantage of the K-nearest neighbors technique is that it offers a rapid time to process, which implies an alleviation of computational processing requirements [34]. This observation suggests that the

K-nearest neighbors machine learning algorithm is a plausible candidate for both Cloud computing and Fog computing scenarios.

The origins of the K-nearest neighbors derive from the 1950s with a statistical emphasis [45, 46]. This technique is considered an instance-based machine learning algorithm, and the algorithm utilizes a distance metric, such as a Euclidean distance. A new instance is allocated to a class comprising a majority of the closest k-neighbors, which for a feature set defined by numeric attributes may be established by distance-weighted averages [47].

The K-nearest neighbors is accessed by the **Classify** panel of the Weka Explorer. Select the **Choose** icon inside the **Classifier** section for the **Classify** panel. Within the available classifiers is the **lazy** file structure and **IBk** that represents the K-nearest neighbors machine learning algorithm. The process for selecting the K-nearest neighbors represented in Figure 6.10 [37–39].

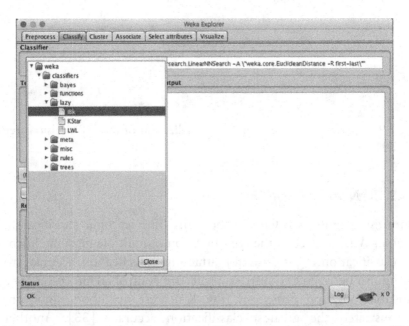

Fig. 6.10. Process for selecting the K-nearest neighbors using the Weka Explorer [37–39].

6.3.3 *Logistic Regression*

A notable clinical observation is the perspective that certain machine learning classification algorithms are suitable for particular scenarios. However, a single machine learning algorithm may not be recommended for an assortment of disparate research endeavors. For example, the logistic regression machine learning algorithm displays the ability to consider the general perspective of the changes in distribution respective of a specific pathology [14].

A distinctly inherent aspect of the logistic regression algorithm integrated into WEKA is the logit transform. The logit transform is a transformation function that is represented by a sigmoid function [45]. The logistic regression algorithm utilized by WEKA also incorporates the ridge estimator advocated by Le Cessie and Van Houwelingen to protect the classification scenario from overfitting [48, 49]. Overfitting pertains to a machine learning classification algorithm that classifies too specifically to the respective training data [45].

In order to access the logistic regression algorithm through WEKA, select the **Choose** icon within the **Classifier** section of the **Classify** panel encapsulated with the Weka Explorer. The logistic regression is accessed through the **functions** file structure, and **Logistic** represents the logistic regression machine learning classification algorithm. The process for acquiring logistic regression for machine learning classification through WEKA is illustrated in Figure 6.11 [37–39].

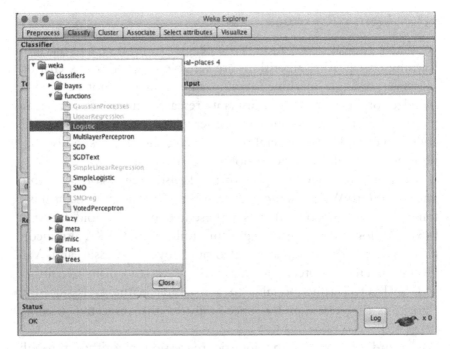

Fig. 6.11. Process for selecting the logistic regression using the Weka Explorer [37–39].

6.3.4 *Naïve Bayes*

The naïve Bayes machine learning classification algorithm incorporates two inherent assumptions. All of the attributes are assumed to serve an equivalent importance for the machine learning classification process. Also, the attributes are assumed to be effectively statistically independent, although this assumption is realized as not being absolutely correct during the application of the naïve Bayes machine learning classification technique [37–39]. In fact, the term "naïve" is applied to the technique, because of the naïve assumption of statistical independence [45]. The foundation for this classification process is the Bayes' theorem [37–39, 45, 50]. The implementation of the naïve Bayes machine learning classification algorithm for WEKA is derived from the research contribution of John and Langley [37–39, 51].

In order to access the naïve Bayes machine learning classification algorithm using WEKA, select the **Choose** icon from the **Classifier** section of the **Classify** panel from within the Weka Explorer. The naïve Bayes is accessed through the **bayes** file structure, and **NaiveBayes** represents the naïve Bayes machine learning classification algorithm. The procedure for accessing the naïve Bayes machine learning classification technique from WEKA is illustrated in Figure 6.12 [37–39].

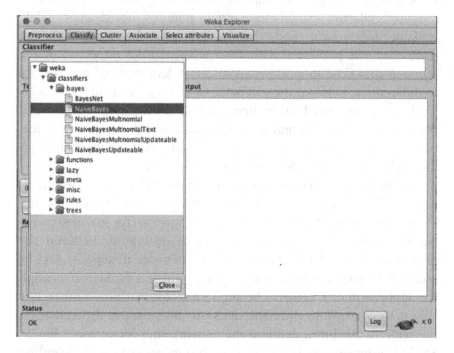

Fig. 6.12.   Process for selecting the naïve Bayes machine learning classification algorithm using the Weka Explorer [37–39].

6.3.5 *Support Vector Machine*

The support vector machine represents a robust classifying algorithm that has been successfully implemented during the preliminary amalgamation of machine learning with wearable and wireless systems. Considerable classification accuracy was attained for distinguishing between a hemiplegic reflex pair respective of the patellar tendon reflex response of a hemiplegic affected leg and unaffected leg. The reflex response was quantified through a portable media device constituting a wearable and wireless accelerometer platform, and the patellar tendon reflex was evoked by a potential energy–derived impact pendulum [13].

Prior to the advent of wearable and wireless inertial sensor systems for gait analysis Begg et al. applied motion analysis cameras with foot mounted reflective markers to ascertain minimal foot clearance while walking for young and elderly subjects. An aspect of the feature set was populated with descriptive statistics respective of the acquired data. The support vector machine demonstrated the capacity to differentiate between the gait patterns of young and elderly subjects [52]. In an associated study, Begg and Kamruzzaman demonstrated the relevance of kinetic and kinematic gait data for composing as feature set to differentiate between young and elderly subjects through the application of a support vector machine [53].

A significant publication regarding the development of the concept of the support vector machine was published by Cortes and Vapnik during the 1990s [54–56]. The support vector machine incorporates a network of support vectors to distinguish between the respective classes of the feature set. The network of support vectors establish a maximum margin hyperplane, which is facilitated through the application of a kernel. The support vector machine is inherently robust to overfitting, since the decision boundary is dependent on the relevant attributes defining the network support vectors [37–39, 54–56]. A hyperplane represents a high-dimensional plane comprised of multiple attributes [47].

The support vector machine implemented by WEKA is based on an algorithm advocated by Platt [37–39]. The new algorithm presented by Platt for training the support vector machine is referred to as sequential minimal optimization (SMO). The SMO algorithm has been demonstrated to be significantly faster than other conventional versions of the support vector machine [57].

The WEKA version of the support vector machine is available by accessing the **Classify** panel through the Weka Explorer. Within the **Classify** panel select the **Choose** icon displayed in the **Classifier** section. The support vector machine is acquired through the **functions** file structure by selecting **SMO,** which is the sequential minimal optimization algorithm advocated by Platt. The scheme for utilizing the WEKA support vector machine for machine learning classification is demonstrated in Figure 6.13 [37–39].

With the support vector machine selected multiple kernel functions are available. The kernel function may be specified through right-clicking the SMO algorithm to the right of the **Choose** icon and selecting **Show properties**. The **weka.gui.GenericObjectEditor** window appears with the **Choose** icon to the right of the **kernel**

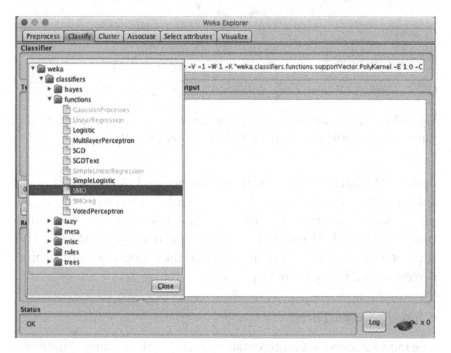

Fig. 6.13. Approach for selecting the support vector machine using the Weka Explorer [37–39].

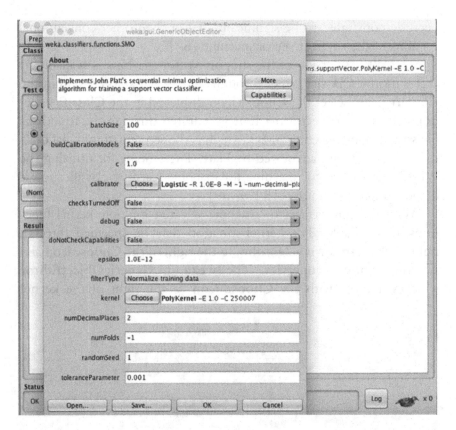

Fig. 6.14. Approach for selecting the kernels to be implemented in the support vector machine using the Weka Explorer [37–39].

option. The default is the polynomial kernel, and other kernels available are the normalized polynomial kernel, precomputed kernel matrix kernel, Pearson VII function–based universal kernel, radial basis function (RBF) kernel, and subsequence kernel (SSK). The approach for selecting a specific kernel for the support vector machine is represented in Figure 6.14 [37–39].

6.3.6 *Random Forest*

The random forest is a representation of ensemble learning. Ensemble learning incorporates an amalgamation of machine learning algorithms. The advantage is the potential to advance the classification accuracy. However, an inherent disadvantage is that the output product can be challenging to interpret [58].

The random forest incorporates the fundamentals of the decision tree algorithm, which is representative of the J48 decision tree perspective. The algorithm is randomized. By contrast, the J48 decision tree emphasizes the most appropriate attribute to branch in the respective decision tree. Instead of selecting the optimal attribute, the random forest algorithm selects a few attributes through randomization. In general, a random assortment of decision trees enables an improvement in performance to be attained [37–39]. The random forest algorithm advocated by WEKA is developed by the research of Breiman [59].

Through WEKA, the random forest machine algorithm can be selected through the **trees** file structure by choosing **RandomForest**. This pathway is provided through the Weka Explorer **Classify** panel using the **Choose** icon in the **Classifier** panel. The approach for acquiring the WEKA random forest machine learning classification algorithm is provided by Figure 6.15 [37–39].

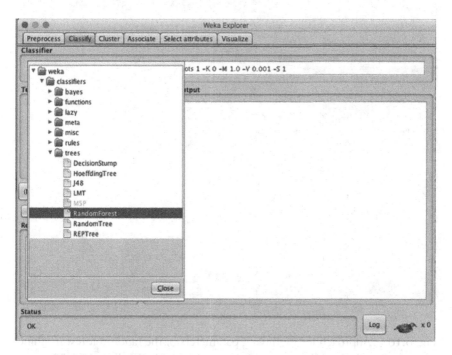

Fig. 6.15.   The pathway for accessing random forest using WEKA [37–39].

There are multiple parameters that may be varied at the discretion of the machine learning research team. These parameters may be considered through right-clicking the random forest algorithm to the right of the **Choose** icon and selecting **Show properties**. Right-clicking the random forest algorithm to the right of the **Choose** icon opens the **weka.gui.GenericObjectEditor** window that provides access to these parameters for defining the operation of the random forest machine learning algorithm. The maximum depth of the decision trees (**maxDepth**) is set by default to **0** for an unlimited depth. The number of features (**numFeatures**) is number of attributes used in the random selection, such as **3** for the top three attributes. The process for modifying random forest parameters using WEKA is illustrated in Figure 6.16 [37–39].

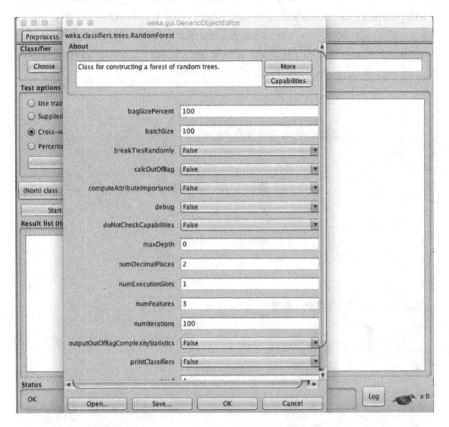

Fig. 6.16.   Approach for modifying parameters of the random forest machine learning classification algorithm throughout the Weka Explorer [37–39].

6.3.7 *Multilayer Perceptron Neural Network*

Intuitively the brain is uniquely endowed with the ability to classify a complex task. The characteristic foundation of the brain is revealed through the neuron. However, the intrinsic neuronal level does not solely achieve the capacity to elicit classification. The interconnectivity of a considerable array of neural networks establish the ability to classify the respective environment. With this observation, the subject of developing artificial neural networks for attaining machine learning classification is a notable endeavor of interest [56].

In order to address the concept of an artificial neural network, a perspective of the anatomy of the neuron is relevant. There are three essential elements that comprise the neuron: the dendrites, soma, and axon. The role of the dendrites is to receive neural signal input, which is integrated at the soma that constitutes the body of the neuron. From the soma the neural signal is conveyed through the axon. The plasticity of the neuron, which signifies the relative proclivity to adaptation, occurs through the modification of the dendritic structure. Figure 6.17 illustrates the general structure of the neuron [60, 61].

In order to emulate the neuron, the artificial neural network is comprised of three aspects known as layers: the input layer, hidden layer, and output layer. For the artificial neural network, the input layer involves the attributes that compose the feature set. The hidden layer receives weighted input from the input layer to generate an output layer [56, 62]. With respect to the multilayer perceptron neural network algorithm utilized by WEKA, the number of hidden layer

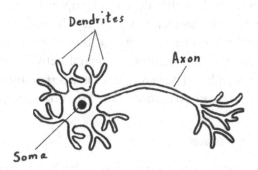

Fig. 6.17. The fundamental neuron consisting of dendrites, soma, and axon [60, 61].

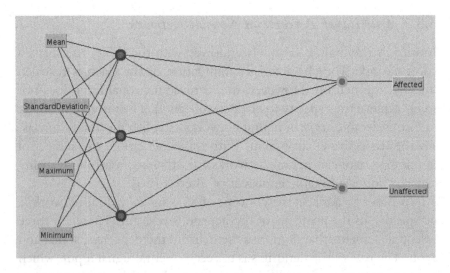

Fig. 6.18. A generic neural network (representative of distinguishing reduced arm swing) composed of an input layer, hidden layer, and output layer [21, 37–39].

nodes is the mean of the sum of the total of input layer nodes and output layer nodes [37–39].

The input layer is representative of the dendrites, for which the hidden layer signifies the soma, and the output layer is comparative to the axonal output. The output layer pertains to the respective classes to be distinguished through machine learning classification. A generic neural network is presented in Figure 6.18 [56, 60–62].

Through WEKA, the multilayer perceptron neural network machine learning classification algorithm develops an optimal neural network for achieving a respective classification accuracy. In order to achieve this objective, two inherent characteristics of the neural network must be realized: the structure that defines the neural network and the associated connection weights. The algorithm for ascertaining the weights of a defined neural network structure is known as backpropagation [56].

6.3.7.1 *Backpropagation*

This algorithm incorporates error that is backpropagated from the output layer to hidden layer [63]. This technique was first advocated by Bryson and Ho during 1969 [63, 64]. During the decade of the 1980s, the concept of backpropagation was amalgamated in the application of neural networks [65].

Backpropagation incorporates the use of a technique known as gradient descent, which is an algorithm applied for optimization. The gradient descent algorithm requires the application of derivatives. This requirement prevents the incorporation of a simple step function (0 and 1), since such a function is not differentiable. An alternative function that achieves the criteria of being resemblant of the binary step function and still differentiable would be desirable [56].

These criteria are achieved through the application of the sigmoid function. The sigmoid function displays the capability of converging to zero for large negative inputs and one for large positive inputs. The sigmoid function is presented in equation format in Figure 6.19 and in graphical representation in Figure 6.20 [56].

$$f(x) = \frac{1}{1 + e^{-x}}$$

Fig. 6.19. The equation format of the sigmoid function [56].

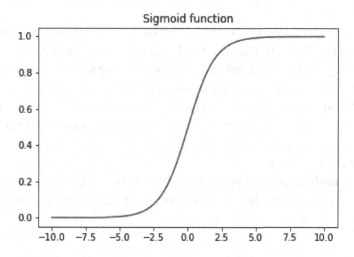

Fig. 6.20. The graphical version of the sigmoid function [56].

6.3.7.2 *Additional Perspectives for the Multilayer Perceptron Neural Network*

The multilayer perceptron neural network is a highly prevalent version of the neural network. This type of neural network is classified as a feed-forward network. The feed-forward network is not characterized as cyclical, and the output is regulated by the current input instance. By contrast, the recurrent neural network demonstrates cyclical capability, for which feedback to the neural network is incorporated from computational contributions established by previous input. This capability attributes the recurrent neural network with a semblance of memory [56].

There are inherent drawbacks to the multilayer perceptron neural network, such as the nature of the conventional gradient descent algorithm, which has been observed as protracted. Another issue with this type of machine learning algorithm is opacity of the resultant machine learning model [56]. This observation is especially relevant to the domain of enhancing clinical acuity for the augmented diagnosis and prognosis of human health status. Especially for scenarios without pressing temporal constraints, the multilayer perceptron neural network has been successfully demonstrated to attain considerable classification accuracy respective of preliminary human health status distinction [4–12, 18, 20–25, 27–32, 34–36].

Obtaining the multilayer perceptron neural network is achieved through the **Classify** panel of the Weka Explorer. The **Classifier** section of the respective panel includes the **Choose** icon consisting of an assortment of classifiers. This classifier is comprised within the **functions** file structure, and **MultilayerPerceptron** enables the multilayer perceptron neural network. A representative screen capture for accessing the multilayer perceptron neural network is presented in Figure 6.21 [37–39].

The multilayer perceptron neural network can be visualized at the discretion of the machine learning research team, and the process is

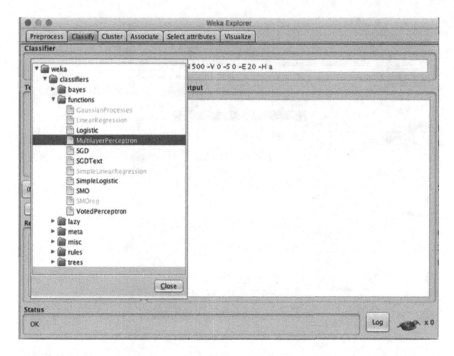

Fig. 6.21. Process for accessing the multilayer perceptron neural network through the Weka Explorer [37–39].

demonstrated in Figure 6.22. In order to visualize the multilayer perceptron neural network, right-click about the field to the right of the **Choose** icon and then select **Show properties**, which opens the **weka.gui.GenericObjectEditor** window. Modify the **GUI** pull-down box to **True**. Clicking the **Start** button above the **Result list** section of the **Classify** panel will generate a representative multilayer perceptron neural network [37–39].

Figure 6.23 displays a representative multilayer perceptron neural network. Note the input layer to the left aspect represents the number of numeric attributes that comprise the feature set. The output layer situated to the right aspect of Figure 6.23 is equivalent to the number of classes involved in the machine

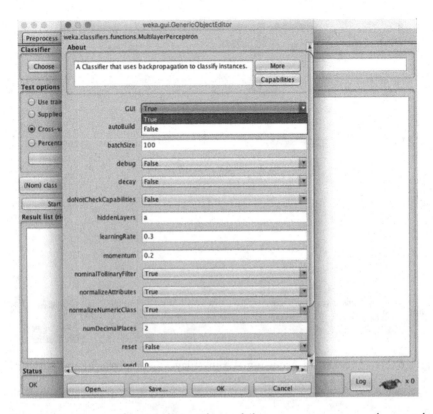

Fig. 6.22. Process for visualizing the multilayer perceptron neural network [37–39].

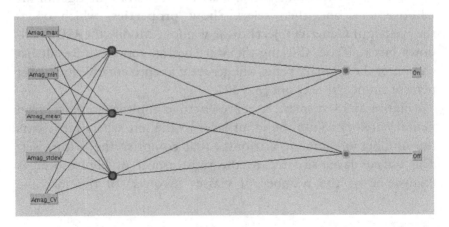

Fig. 6.23. A representative multilayer perceptron neural network [37–39].

learning classification endeavor. The number of hidden layers situated in the middle of the multilayer perceptron neural network is derived from the summed average of the input layer and output layer [37–39].

Further inspection of the parameters available in Figure 6.22 reveals other opportunities to refine the specificity of the multilayer perceptron neural network. Within the **weka.gui.GenericObjectEditor** window the organization of the hidden layer(s) of the multilayer perceptron neural network can be modified through the **hiddenLayers** field. For example, enter **5, 10, 20** into the **hiddenLayers** field as demonstrated in Figure 6.24. The result is presented in Figure 6.25,

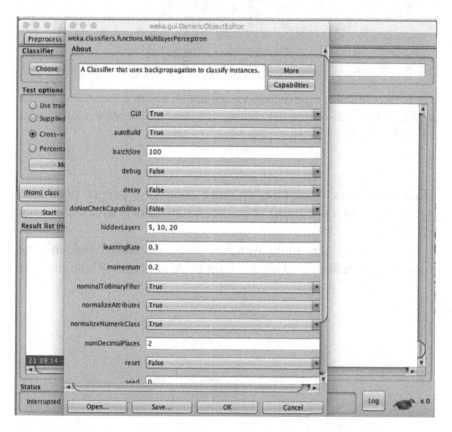

Fig. 6.24. The process for assigning a specific organization of the hidden layer aspect of the multilayer perceptron neural network [37–39].

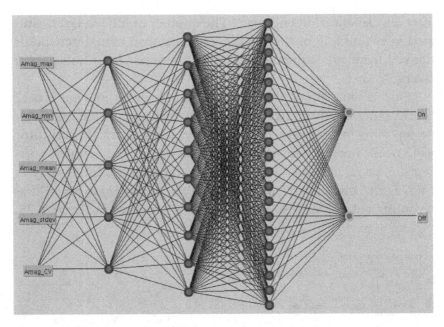

Fig. 6.25. Multilayer perceptron neural network with a specified sequence of hidden layers consisting of columns of 5, 10, and 20 hidden layer nodes from left to right [37–39].

which represents a considerably more complex sequence of hidden layers consisting of columns of 5, 10, and 20 hidden layer nodes from left to right [37–39].

Furthermore, the multilayer perceptron neural network may be manually assigned a novel hidden layer node structure. Right-click the

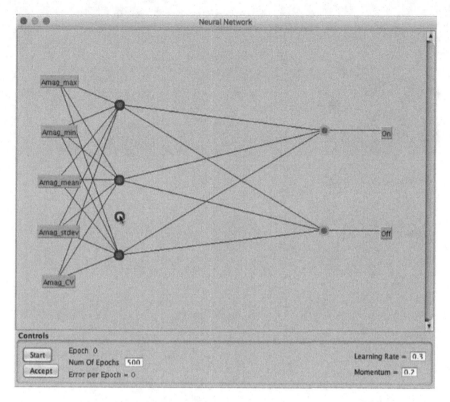

Fig. 6.26. Procedure for assigning a new node to the hidden layer of the multilayer perceptron neural network [37–39].

multilayer perceptron neural network as shown in Figure 6.26 for the introduction of a new hidden layer node. Subsequently, with the new hidden layer node selected, connect the new hidden layer node to the

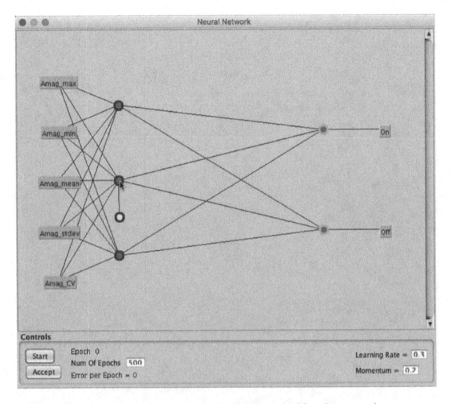

Fig. 6.27. Procedure for connecting the new hidden layer node to a preliminary hidden layer node [37–39].

appropriate associated nodes as demonstrated in Figures 6.27 through 6.29 [37–39].

There are three additional parameters that may be modified to influence the development of the multilayer perceptron neural network:

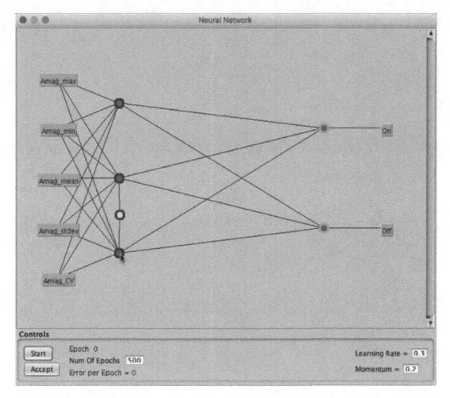

Fig. 6.28. Procedure for connecting the new hidden layer node to a secondary hidden layer node [37–39].

learning rate, momentum, and **training time**. The **learning rate** and **momentum** influence the progressive modification of the multilayer perceptron neural network weights. The **training time** represents the

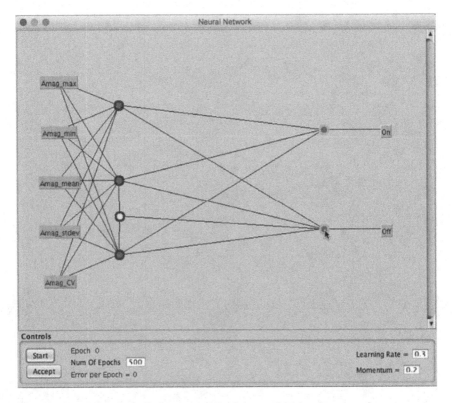

Fig. 6.29. Procedure for connecting the new hidden layer node to an output layer node [37–39].

number of epochs (iterations) through the backpropagation process. Figure 6.30 demonstrates the process for modifying **learning rate**, **momentum**, and **training time** of the multilayer perceptron neural network through accessing the **weka.gui.GenericObjectEditor** window by right-clicking about the field to the right of the **Choose** icon and then selecting **Show properties**. For Figure 6.30 the **learning rate** is set to 0.3; **momentum** is set to 0.2; and **training time** is set to 500 epochs [37–39].

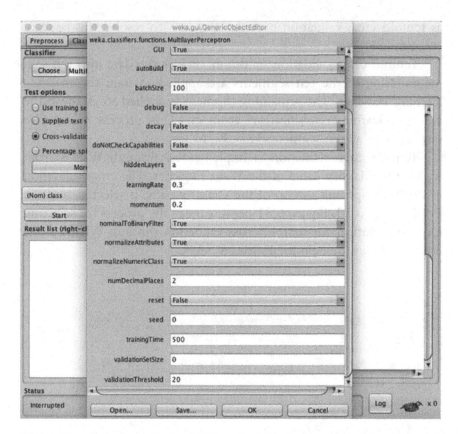

Fig. 6.30. Procedure for modifying the **learning rate**, **momentum**, and **training time** for the multilayer perceptron neural network [37–39].

6.4 Test Options for Machine Learning Classification

The type of machine learning classification that is advocated is known as supervised learning. Supervised learning involves machine learning classification with the output defined. Unsupervised learning pertains to a scenario that involves the output not being established [37–39, 66].

Intuitively, supervised learning inherently warrants the concern of simultaneously training and testing with respect to the same feature set. Such an approach may call into question the veracity of the attained machine learning classification accuracy. A concept known as tenfold cross-validation provides a means to resolve this issue of concern [37–39].

Tenfold cross-validation randomly divides the data into ten segments. Nine of the ten segments are applied to train the machine learning classifier. The remaining segment is applied to establish the machine learning classification accuracy. This process is iterative respective of all ten segments [37–39, 67].

Tenfold cross-validation is implemented through WEKA from within the **Classify** panel of the Weka Explorer. The cross-validation in the **Test options** section of the **Classify** panel is selected, and the **Folds** is set to 10. Figure 6.31 demonstrates the process for selecting **Cross-validation** for tenfold cross-validation through WEKA while entering **10** in the field for **Folds** [37–39].

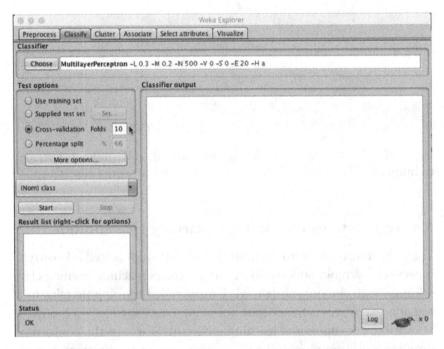

Fig. 6.31. Selecting tenfold cross-validation through WEKA [37–39].

6.5 Classifier Output for Machine Learning Classification

Upon selecting the **Start** button above the **Result list** section of the **Classify** panel, a machine learning classification accuracy is attained based on the selected machine learning algorithm. The **Classifier output** section presents the results of the machine learning classification algorithm as featured in Figure 6.32. Each algorithm provides standard results to ascertain the performance of the machine learning classification algorithm:

(1) Classification accuracy (Correctly classified instances)
(2) Confusion matrix
(3) Time taken to build model

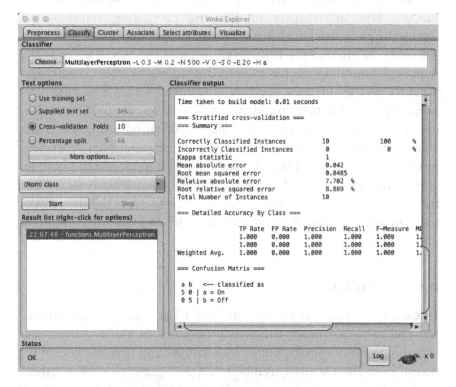

Fig. 6.32. The **Classifier output** section presenting the results of the machine learning classification algorithm [37–39].

Classification accuracy represents the percentage of correctly classified instances, and below is the percentage of incorrectly classified instances. The confusion matrix provides enhanced insight with respect to the nature of the classification accuracy. In fact, for a binary (two classes composing the feature set) classification scenario, multiple machine learning classification algorithms can attain the same classification accuracy. However, the manner that these algorithms achieve the same classification may actually be disparate, for which the confusion matrix can elucidate this distinction. The confusion matrix presents the number of correctly and incorrectly classified instances respective of both classes. For a binary machine learning classification scenario, the confusion matrix is presented as a two-by-two matrix [37–39].

Another important parameter acquired is the time taken to build model. This information implies the processing requirements imposed by the machine learning classification algorithm. One consideration is whether the time taken to build the model exceeds any temporal bounding requirements. Regardless of the classification accuracy, the results may need to be resolved within a specific temporal window. Another consideration is with respect to the possibility of conducting machine learning classification using the same algorithm with a system that has reduced computational processing power, for which the time taken to build the model would have an amplified impact. This observation would be particularly significant for advanced wearable and wireless systems that locally achieve machine learning classification accuracy, such as for a Fog computing architecture [31].

6.6 Conclusion

In Chapter 5 'Automation of Feature Set Extraction using Python', the ability to automate the post-processing of the accelerometer signal data from a smartphone as a wearable and wireless system for quantifying the essential tremor reach and grasp task with respect to deep brain stimulation set to 'On' and 'Off' has been achieved. With the ability to derive the ARFF file through the automated post-processing of Python software, the application of WEKA for conducting machine learning classification has been thoroughly addressed.

An operational perspective of WEKA has been discussed, such as the opening of WEKA and upload of an ARFF file for machine learning classification. The process for accessing seven machine learning algorithms has been presented:

(1) J48 decision tree
(2) K-nearest neighbors
(3) Logistic regression
(4) Naïve Bayes
(5) Support vector machine
(6) Random forest
(7) Multilayer perceptron neural network

In addition to a synopsis of the fundamental basis for their machine learning algorithms, the general procedure for the operation of these seven machine learning algorithms has been discussed in detail. These subjects enable the ability to evolve to Chapter 7 'Machine Learning Classification of Essential Tremor using a Reach and Grasp Task with Deep Brain Stimulation System Set to 'On' and 'Off' Status' for assessing the performance characteristics of these seven machine learning algorithms that are an aspect of the WEKA machine learning platform.

References

1. LeMoyne, R., Tomycz, N., Mastroianni, T., McCandless, C., Cozza, M. and Peduto, D. (2015). Implementation of a smartphone wireless accelerometer platform for establishing deep brain stimulation treatment efficacy of essential tremor with machine learning, *Proc. 37th Annual International Conference of the IEEE, Engineering in Medicine and Biology Society (EMBS)*, pp. 6772–6775.
2. LeMoyne, R., Coroian, C., Mastroianni, T., Opalinski, P., Cozza, M. and Grundfest W. (2009). *Biomedical Engineering*, ed. Barros de

Mello, C. A., Chapter 10 "The Merits of Artificial Proprioception, with Applications in Biofeedback Gait Rehabilitation Concepts and Movement Disorder Characterization," (InTech, Vienna), pp. 165–198.

3. LeMoyne, R. and Mastroianni, T. (2015). *Mobile Health Technologies, Methods and Protocols*, eds. Rasooly, A. and Herold, K. E., Chapter 23 "Use of Smartphones and Portable Media Devices for Quantifying Human Movement Characteristics of Gait, Tendon Reflex Response, and Parkinson's Disease Hand Tremor," (Springer, New York) pp. 335–358.

4. LeMoyne, R. and Mastroianni, T. (2016). *Telemedicine*, "Telemedicine Perspectives for Wearable and Wireless Applications Serving the Domain of Neurorehabilitation and Movement Disorder Treatment," (SMGroup, Dover) pp. 1–10.

5. LeMoyne, R. and Mastroianni, T. (2017). *Wireless MEMS Networks and Applications*, ed. Uttamchandani, D., Chapter 6 "Wearable and Wireless Gait Analysis Platforms: Smartphones and Portable Media Devices," (Elsevier, New York) pp. 129–152.

6. LeMoyne, R. and Mastroianni, T. (2017). *Smartphones from an Applied Research Perspective*, ed. Mohamudally, N., Chapter 1 "Smartphone and Portable Media Device: A Novel Pathway toward the Diagnostic Characterization of Human Movement," (InTech, Rijeka) pp. 1–24.

7. LeMoyne, R. and Mastroianni, T. (2018). *Wearable and Wireless Systems for Healthcare I: Gait and Reflex Response Quantification*, (Springer, Singapore).

8. LeMoyne, R. and Mastroianni, T. (2018). *Wearable and Wireless Systems for Healthcare I: Gait and Reflex Response Quantification*, Chapter 9 "Role of Machine Learning for Gait and Reflex Response Classification," (Springer, Singapore) pp. 111–120.

9. LeMoyne, R., Mastroianni, T., Whiting, D. and Tomycz, N. (2019). *Wearable and Wireless Systems for Healthcare II: Movement Disorder Evaluation and Deep Brain Stimulation Systems*, (Springer, Singapore).

10. LeMoyne, R., Mastroianni, T., Whiting, D. and Tomycz, N. (2019). *Wearable and Wireless Systems for Healthcare II: Movement Disorder Evaluation and Deep Brain Stimulation Systems*, Chapter 8 "Role of Machine Learning for Classification of Movement Disorder and Deep Brain Stimulation Status," (Springer, Singapore) pp. 99–111.

11. LeMoyne, R. and Mastroianni, T. (2019). *Smartphones: Recent Innovations and Applications*, ed. Dabove, P., Chapter 7 "Network Centric Therapy for Wearable and Wireless Systems," (Nova Science Publishers, Hauppauge).

12. LeMoyne, R. and Mastroianni, T. (2020). *Multilayer Perceptrons: Theory and Applications*, ed. Vang-Mata, R., Chapter 2 "Machine Learning Classification for Network Centric Therapy Utilizing the Multilayer Perceptron Neural Network," (Nova Science Publishers, Hauppauge) pp. 39–76.

13. LeMoyne, R., Kerr, W., Zanjani, K. and Mastroianni, T. (2014). Implementation of an iPod wireless accelerometer application using machine learning to classify disparity of hemiplegic and healthy patellar tendon reflex pair, *J. Med. Imaging Health Inform.*, 4, pp. 21–28.

14. LeMoyne, R., Kerr, W., Mastroianni, T. and Hessel, A. (2014). Implementation of machine learning for classifying hemiplegic gait disparity through use of a force plate, *Proc. 13th International Conference on Machine Learning and Applications (ICMLA), IEEE*, pp. 379–382.

15. LeMoyne, R., Mastroianni, T., Hessel, A. and Nishikawa, K. (2015). Implementation of machine learning for classifying prosthesis type through conventional gait analysis, *Proc. 37th Annual International Conference of the IEEE, Engineering in Medicine and Biology Society (EMBS)*, pp. 202–205.

16. LeMoyne, R. and Mastroianni, T. (2015). Machine learning classification of a hemiplegic and healthy patellar tendon reflex pair through an iPod wireless gyroscope platform, *Proc. 45th Society for Neuroscience Annual Meeting*.

17. LeMoyne, R., Kerr, W. and Mastroianni, T. (2015). Implementation of machine learning with an iPod application mounted to cane for classifying assistive device usage, *J. Med. Imaging Health Inform.*, 5, pp. 1404–1408.

18. LeMoyne, R., Mastroianni, T., Hessel, A. and Nishikawa, K. (2015). Application of a multilayer perceptron neural network for classifying software platforms of a powered prosthesis through a force plate, *Proc. 14th International Conference on Machine Learning and Applications (ICMLA), IEEE*, pp. 402–405.

19. LeMoyne, R., Mastroianni, T., Hessel, A. and Nishikawa, K. (2015). Ankle rehabilitation system with feedback from a smartphone wire-

less gyroscope platform and machine learning classification, *Proc. 14th International Conference on Machine Learning and Applications (ICMLA), IEEE*, pp. 406–409.

20. LeMoyne, R., Heerinckx, F., Aranca, T., De Jager, R., Zesiewicz, T. and Saal, H. J. (2016). Wearable body and wireless inertial sensors for machine learning classification of gait for people with Friedreich's ataxia, *Proc. 13th Annual International Body Sensor Networks Conference (BSN), IEEE*, pp. 147–151.

21. LeMoyne, R. and Mastroianni, T. (2016). Implementation of a smartphone as a wireless gyroscope platform for quantifying reduced arm swing in hemiplegic gait with machine learning classification by multilayer perceptron neural network, *Proc. 38th Annual International Conference of the IEEE, Engineering in Medicine and Biology Society (EMBS)*, pp. 2626–2630.

22. LeMoyne, R. and Mastroianni, T. (2016). Smartphone wireless gyroscope platform for machine learning classification of hemiplegic patellar tendon reflex pair disparity through a multilayer perceptron neural network, *Proc. Wireless Health (WH), IEEE*, pp. 1–6.

23. LeMoyne, R. and Mastroianni, T. (2016). Implementation of a multilayer perceptron neural network for classifying a hemiplegic and healthy reflex pair using an iPod wireless gyroscope platform, *Proc. 46th Society for Neuroscience Annual Meeting*.

24. LeMoyne, R. and Mastroianni, T. (2017). Virtual proprioception for eccentric training, *Proc. 39th Annual International Conference of the IEEE, Engineering in Medicine and Biology Society (EMBS)*, pp. 4557–4561.

25. LeMoyne, R. and Mastroianni, T. (2017). Wireless gyroscope platform enabled by a portable media device for quantifying wobble board therapy, *Proc. 39th Annual International Conference of the IEEE, Engineering in Medicine and Biology Society (EMBS)*, pp. 2662–2666.

26. LeMoyne, R. and Mastroianni, T. (2017). Implementation of a smartphone wireless gyroscope platform with machine learning for classifying disparity of a hemiplegic patellar tendon reflex pair, *J. Mech. Med. Biol.*, 17, 1750083.

27. LeMoyne, R., Mastroianni, T., Tomycz, N., Whiting, D., Oh, M., McCandless, C., Currivan, C. and Peduto, D. (2017). Implementation

of a multilayer perceptron neural network for classifying deep brain stimulation in 'On' and 'Off' modes through a smartphone representing a wearable and wireless sensor application, *Proc. 47th Society for Neuroscience Annual Meeting, featured in Hot Topics (top 1% of abstracts).*

28. LeMoyne, R., Mastroianni, T., McCandless, C., Currivan, C., Whiting, D. and Tomycz, N. (2018). Implementation of a smartphone as a wearable and wireless accelerometer and gyroscope platform for ascertaining deep brain stimulation treatment efficacy of Parkinson's disease through machine learning classification, *Adv. Park. Dis.*, 7, pp. 19–30.

29. LeMoyne, R., Mastroianni, T., McCandless, C., Currivan, C., Whiting, D. and Tomycz, N. (2018). Implementation of a smartphone as a wearable and wireless inertial sensor platform for determining efficacy of deep brain stimulation for Parkinson's disease tremor through machine learning, *Proc. 48th Society for Neuroscience Annual Meeting, Nanosymposium.*

30. LeMoyne, R. and Mastroianni, T. (2018). Implementation of a smartphone as a wearable and wireless gyroscope platform for machine learning classification of hemiplegic gait through a multilayer perceptron neural network, *Proc. 17th International Conference on Machine Learning and Applications (ICMLA), IEEE,* pp. 946–950.

31. LeMoyne, R., Mastroianni, T., Whiting, D. and Tomycz, N. (2019). *Wearable and Wireless Systems for Healthcare II: Movement Disorder Evaluation and Deep Brain Stimulation Systems,* Chapter 9 "Assessment of Machine Learning Classification Strategies for the Differentiation of Deep Brain Stimulation "On" and "Off" Status for Parkinson's Disease Using a Smartphone as a Wearable and Wireless Inertial Sensor for Quantified Feedback," (Springer, Singapore) pp. 113–126.

32. LeMoyne, R., Mastroianni, T., McCandless, C., Whiting, D. and Tomycz, N. (2019). Evaluation of machine learning algorithms for classifying deep brain stimulation respective of 'On' and 'Off' status, *Proc. 9th International IEEE Conference on Neural Engineering (NER), IEEE/EMBS,* pp. 483–488.

33. LeMoyne, R. and Mastroianni, T. (2019). Classification of software control architectures for a powered prosthesis through conventional gait analysis using machine learning applications, *J. Mech. Med. Biol.,* 19, 1950044.

34. LeMoyne, R., Mastroianni, T., Whiting, D. and Tomycz, N. (2019). Network Centric Therapy for deep brain stimulation status parametric analysis with machine learning classification, *Proc. 49th Society for Neuroscience Annual Meeting, Nanosymposium*.

35. LeMoyne, R., Mastroianni, T., Whiting, D. and Tomycz, N. (2019). Preliminary Network Centric Therapy for machine learning classification of deep brain stimulation status for the treatment of Parkinson's disease with a conformal wearable and wireless inertial sensor, *Adv. Park. Dis.*, 8, pp. 75–91.

36. Mastroianni, T. and LeMoyne, R. (2016). Application of a multilayer perceptron neural network with an iPod as a wireless gyroscope platform to classify reduced arm swing gait for people with Erb's palsy, *Proc. 46th Society for Neuroscience Annual Meeting*.

37. Hall, M., Frank, E., Holmes, G., Pfahringer, B., Reutemann, P. and Witten I. H. (2009). The WEKA data mining software: An update, *ACM SIGKDD Explor. Newsl.*, 11, pp. 10–18.

38. Witten, I. H., Frank, E. and Hall, M. A. (2011). *Data Mining: Practical Machine Learning Tools and Techniques*, 3rd Ed. (Morgan Kaufmann Publishers, Burlington).

39. WEKA [www.cs.waikato.ac.nz/~ml/weka/]

40. Quinlan, J. R. (1993). *C4.5 Programs for Machine Learning*, Chapter 1 "Introduction," (Morgan Kaufmann Publishers, San Mateo) pp. 1–16.

41. Quinlan, J. R. (1993). *C4.5: Programs for Machine Learning*, (Morgan Kaufmann Publishers, San Mateo).

42. Quinlan, J. R. (1986). Induction of decision trees, *Mach. Learn.*, 1, pp. 81–106.

43. Wu, X., Kumar, V., Quinlan, J. R., Ghosh, J., Yang, Q., Motoda, H., McLachlan, G. J., Ng, A., Liu, B., Philip, S. Y. and Zhou, Z. H. (2008). Top 10 algorithms in data mining, *Knowl. Inf. Syst.*, 14, pp. 1–37.

44. Harrington, P. (2012). *Machine Learning in Action*, Chapter 3 "Splitting Datasets One Feature at a Time: Decision Trees," (Manning Publications, Shelter Island) pp. 37–60.

45. Witten, I. H., Frank, E. and Hall, M. A. (2011). *Data Mining: Practical Machine Learning Tools and Techniques*, 3rd Ed., Chapter 4 "Algorithms: The Basic Methods," (Morgan Kaufmann Publishers, Burlington) pp. 85–145.

46. Fix, E. and Hodges Jr., J. L. (1951). Discriminatory analysis; non-parametric discrimination: Consistency properties, USAF School of

Aviation Medicine, Randolph Field. Project Number 21-49-004, Report Number 4.

47. Witten, I. H., Frank, E. and Hall, M. A. (2011). *Data Mining: Practical Machine Learning Tools and Techniques*, 3rd Ed., Chapter 3 "Output: Knowledge Representation," (Morgan Kaufmann Publishers, Burlington) pp. 61–83.

48. Witten, I. H., Frank, E. and Hall, M. A. (2011). *Data Mining: Practical Machine Learning Tools and Techniques*, 3rd Ed., Chapter 11 "The Explorer," (Morgan Kaufmann Publishers, Burlington) pp. 407–494.

49. Le Cessie, S. and Van Houwelingen, J. C. (1992). Ridge estimators in logistic regression, *J. Royal Stat. Soc.: Ser. C (Appl. Stat.)*, 41, pp. 191–201.

50. Bayes, T. (1763). LII. An essay towards solving a problem in the doctrine of chances. By the late Rev. Mr. Bayes, FRS communicated by Mr. Price, in a letter to John Canton, *AMFR S. Philos. Trans. Royal Soc. Lond.*, 53, pp. 370–418.

51. John, G. H. and Langley, P. (1995). Estimating continuous distributions in Bayesian classifiers, *Proc. 11th Conference on Uncertainty in Artificial Intelligence*.

52. Begg, R. K., Palaniswami, M. and Owen, B. (2005). Support vector machines for automated gait classification, *IEEE Trans. Biomed. Eng.*, 52, pp. 828–838.

53. Begg, R. and Kamruzzaman, J. (2005). A machine learning approach for automated recognition of movement patterns using basic, kinetic and kinematic gait data, *J. Biomech.*, 38, pp. 401–408.

54. Cortes, C. and Vapnik, V. (1995). Support vector networks, *Mach. Learn.*, 20, pp. 273–297.

55. Vapnik, V. N. (1999). *The Nature of Statistical Learning Theory*, 2nd Ed. (Springer-Verlag, New York).

56. Witten, I. H., Frank, E. and Hall, M. A. (2011). *Data Mining: Practical Machine Learning Tools and Techniques*, 3rd Ed., Chapter 6 "Implementations: Real Machine Learning Schemes," (Morgan Kaufmann Publishers, Burlington) pp. 191–304.

57. Platt, J. C. (1999). *Advances in Kernel Methods: Support Vector Learning*, eds. Schölkopf, B., Burges J. C. and Smola, A. J., Chapter 12 "Fast Training of Support Vector Machines using Sequential Minimal Optimization," (The MIT Press Cambridge, Massachusetts) pp. 185–208.

58. Witten, I. H., Frank, E. and Hall, M. A. (2011). *Data Mining: Practical Machine Learning Tools and Techniques*, 3rd Ed., Chapter 8 "Ensemble Learning," (Morgan Kaufmann Publishers, Burlington) pp. 351–373.

59. Breiman, L. (2001). Random forests, *Mach. Learn.*, 45, pp. 5–32.

60. Kandel, E. R., Schwartz, J. H. and Jessell, T. M. (2000). *Principles of Neural Science*, 4th Ed., Chapter 2 "Nerve Cells and Behavior," (McGraw-Hill, New York) pp. 19–35.

61. Seeley, R. R., Stephens, T. D. and Tate, P. (2003). *Anatomy and Physiology*, 6th Ed., Chapter 11 "Function and Organization of Nervous Tissue," (McGraw-Hill, Boston) pp. 363–399.

62. Munakata, T. (2008). *Fundamentals of the New Artificial Intelligence: Neural, Evolutionary, Fuzzy and More*, 2nd Ed., Chapter 2 "Neural Networks: Fundamentals and the Backpropagation Model," (Springer, London) pp. 7–36.

63. Russell S. J. and Norvig P. (2010). *Artificial Intelligence: A Modern Approach*, 3rd Ed., Chapter 18 "Learning from Examples," (Prentice Hall, Upper Saddle River) pp. 693–767.

64. Bryson, A. E. and Ho Y. C. (1969). *Applied Optimal Control: Optimization, Estimation, and Control*, (Blaisdell Publishing, Waltham).

65. Russell S. J. and Norvig P. (2010). *Artificial Intelligence: A Modern Approach*, 3rd Ed., Chapter 1 "Introduction," (Prentice Hall, Upper Saddle River) pp. 1–33.

66. Witten, I. H., Frank, E. and Hall, M. A. (2011). *Data Mining: Practical Machine Learning Tools and Techniques*, 3rd Ed., Chapter 2 "Input: Concepts, Instances, and Attributes," (Morgan Kaufmann Publishers, Burlington) pp. 39–60.

67. Witten, I. H., Frank, E. and Hall, M. A. (2011). *Data Mining: Practical Machine Learning Tools and Techniques*, 3rd Ed., Chapter 5 "Credibility: Evaluating What's Been Learned," (Morgan Kaufmann Publishers, Burlington) pp. 147–187.

Chapter 7

Machine Learning Classification of Essential Tremor using a Reach and Grasp Task with Deep Brain Stimulation System Set to 'On' and 'Off' Status

7.1 Introduction

A smartphone functioning as a wearable and wireless inertial sensor system using the available accelerometer has successfully quantified the reach and grasp task for essential tremor with respect to the deep brain stimulation system set to 'On' and 'Off' status [1]. The accelerometer signal data as visualized in Chapter 5 'Automation of Feature Set Extraction using Python' displays objectively quantified disparity with respect to the contrast of the data pertaining to the deep brain stimulation system set to 'On' and 'Off'. This observation aligns with the opportunity for applying machine learning, which has been previously recommended and successfully demonstrated for differentiating numerous health status scenarios, such as through the objectively quantified inertial sensor signal data obtained by wearable and wireless inertial sensor systems [1–36].

In light of the predetermined software requirements and established pseudo code, Python has been implemented to consolidate the acquired accelerometer signal data into a feature set suitable for the Waikato Environment for Knowledge Analysis (WEKA) known as an

Attribute-Relation File Format (ARFF). Seven machine learning algorithms provided by WEKA are the subject of the subsequent machine learning classification endeavor in conjunction with tenfold cross-validation:

- J48 decision tree
- K-nearest neighbors
- Logistic regression
- Naïve Bayes
- Support vector machine (applied for IEEE EMBC 2015 conference publication)
- Random forest
- Multilayer perceptron neural network [37–39]

The most generally predominant performance parameter for the derived machine learning model is the classification accuracy. In the event that less than 100% classification accuracy is achieved, the confusion matrix should be addressed. Another highly significant performance parameter is the time for the machine learning model to achieve its classification model [9, 11, 12, 29, 31, 34, 35]. The attributes that compose the feature set may be segregated for further machine learning classification investigation. These performance parameters are considered for the subsequent determination of the most appropriate machine learning algorithm with respect to the reach and grasp task for essential tremor utilizing the deep brain stimulation system set to 'On' and 'Off' status.

7.2 Support Vector Machine

The first machine learning algorithm for consideration is the support vector machine, which was utilized for the IEEE EMBC 2015 conference publication 'Implementation of a smartphone wireless accelerometer platform for establishing deep brain stimulation treatment efficacy of essential tremor with machine learning' by Robert LeMoyne (Ph.D.), Nestor Tomycz (M.D.), Timothy Mastroianni, Cyrus McCandless (Ph.D.), Michael Cozza, and David Peduto

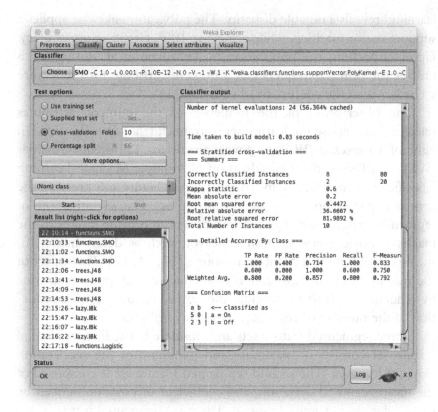

Fig. 7.1. Results of the support vector machine model (full feature set) displayed within the **Classifier output** aspect of the Weka Explorer.

(Lt. Col. Ret.) [1]. Figure 7.1 presents the results machine learning model derived by the support vector machine with the **Classifier output** section of the Weka Explorer. The support vector machine attains 80% classification accuracy. In consideration of the confusion matrix two deep brain stimulation system 'Off' instances are misclassified as deep brain stimulation system set to 'On'. With regard to the temporal performance the model takes 0.03 seconds to develop.

Consultation with the classification accuracy achieved for the IEEE EMBC 2015 conference publication 'Implementation of a smartphone wireless accelerometer platform for establishing deep brain stimulation treatment efficacy of essential tremor with machine learning' reveals a notable disparity. The publication likewise applies a support vector machine, while achieving 100% classification accuracy. Upon inspection, the publication by LeMoyne et al. during 2015 utilizes the primary frequency as a numeric attribute for the feature set rather than the coefficient of variation [1].

The observation of the influence of the numeric attributes selected to compose the feature set warrants further consideration. In light of Chapter 6 'Waikato Environment for Knowledge Analysis (WEKA) a Perspective Consideration of Multiple Machine Learning Classification Algorithms and Applications', Figure 6.5 presents the approach for removing available attributes. The investigation of segmented aspects of the global feature set can provide insight to the machine learning classification endeavor, such as determination of the most predominant numeric attributes [13, 14, 17]. This aspect of the machine learning application can reduce overall processing time by reducing the time to generate the feature set through the reduction of the number of computed numeric attributes.

Three segmented feature sets are considered. The first segmented feature set consists of maximum and minimum of the acceleration magnitude signal. The second segmented feature set is comprised of the mean, standard deviation, and coefficient of variation derived by the acceleration magnitude signal. The third segmented feature set is composed of the maximum and standard deviation based on the acceleration magnitude signal.

For the first segmented feature set (maximum and minimum of the acceleration magnitude signal), the 80% classification accuracy is attained with two instances representing the deep brain stimulation system set to 'Off' status that are misclassified as the deep brain stimulation system set to 'On'. The time to develop the machine learning model is 0.01 seconds. Regarding the second segmented feature set (mean, standard deviation, and coefficient of variation derived by the acceleration magnitude signal), the classification accuracy of 100% is achieved, and the time to converge the machine learning model is reduced to 0.01 seconds. In consideration of the third segmented feature set (maximum and standard deviation based on the acceleration magnitude signal), 80% classification accuracy is achieved and two instances representing the deep brain stimulation system set to 'Off' status are misclassified as the deep brain stimulation system set to 'On', for which the machine learning model takes 0.01 seconds to develop.

These findings for the support vector machine demonstrate the advantages of a reduction in the quantity of numeric attributes to assemble the feature set, for which there are multiple advantages. Intuitively, a reduction in the numeric attributes used to develop the feature set decreases the computational load to post-process the wearable and wireless inertial sensor data. By emphasizing the mean, standard deviation, and coefficient of variation of the acceleration magnitude signal, the classification accuracy is actually improved to 100%. Furthermore, the more concise feature set decreases the time to create the machine learning model by a factor of three to 0.01 seconds. The support vector machine has been applied to numerous occasions for the machine learning classification of human health scenarios with an emphasis toward the application of wearable and wireless inertial sensor systems [1, 6–13, 15, 19, 26, 29, 31–34].

7.3 J48 Decision Tree

In addition to the intrinsic advantages of the J48 decision tree is the utility of visualizing the decision tree. This benefit provides the research team with the opportunity to better understand the role of various numeric attributes for the synergistic derivation of the classification accuracy. Figure 7.2 illustrates the **Classifier output** section of the Weka Explorer for the J48 decision tree for the essential tremor reach and grasp task with the deep brain stimulation system set to 'On' and 'Off' status for the full feature set.

The J48 decision tree achieves 90% classification accuracy, and only one instance of the deep brain stimulation system set to 'On' status is misclassified as being set to 'Off' status. The J48 decision tree machine learning model requires 0.01 seconds to develop. Figure 7.3 represents the derived J48 decision tree, which emphasizes the maximum of the acceleration magnitude for establishing machine learning classification.

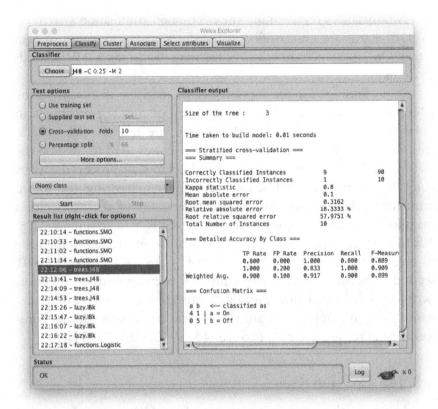

Fig. 7.2.   Results of the J48 decision tree model (full feature set) presented by the **Classifier output** aspect of the Weka Explorer.

Further investigation of the J48 decision tree involves response to the three segmented feature sets. The three segmented feature sets (maximum and minimum of the acceleration magnitude signal), (mean, standard deviation, and coefficient of variation derived by the acceleration magnitude signal), and (maximum and standard deviation based on the acceleration magnitude signal) all achieved 90% classification accuracy with one misclassification of deep brain stimulation system set to 'On' status being mistaken as set to 'Off' status. The reduction of the quantity of numeric attributes for the three segmented feature sets has the influence of reducing the time to develop the model to less than 0.01 seconds. The J48 decision tree has been utilized for the machine learning classification of human

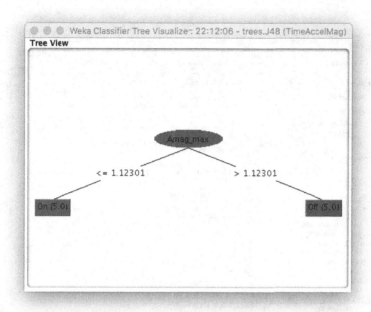

Fig. 7.3. The J48 decision tree derived using the full feature set for differentiating between deep brain stimulation system set to 'On' and 'Off' status regarding the reach and grasp task for essential tremor.

health scenarios regarding an emphasis toward the application of wearable and wireless inertial sensor systems with the additional benefit of providing a visualization of the machine learning process [6–10, 16, 26, 29, 31–34].

7.4 K-Nearest Neighbors

K-nearest neighbors machine learning classification algorithm has been successfully applied to multiple endeavors of distinguishing human health scenarios through objectively quantified sensor signal data, such as through wearable and wireless inertial sensor systems [7–10, 26, 29, 31–34]. Figure 7.4 represents the **Classifier output** section of the Weka Explorer for the K-nearest neighbors utilizing the full feature set with respect to the essential tremor reach and grasp task for the deep brain stimulation system set to 'On' and 'Off' status. The K-nearest

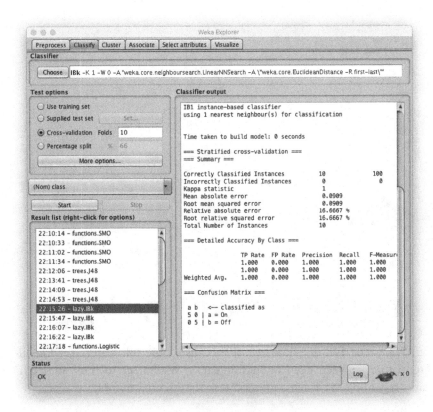

Fig. 7.4. K-nearest neighbors applying the full feature set for distinguishing deep brain stimulation system set to 'On' and 'Off' status regarding the reach and grasp task for essential tremor quantified by the smartphone as a wearable and wireless inertial sensor system.

neighbors attains 100% classification accuracy for distinguishing between the deep brain stimulation system set to 'On' and 'Off' status regarding the essential tremor reach and grasp task incorporating the smartphone as a wearable and wireless inertial sensor system. The K-nearest neighbors machine learning model requires less than 0.01 seconds to develop. With respect to the three segmented feature sets under consideration (maximum and minimum of the acceleration magnitude signal), (mean, standard deviation, and coefficient of variation derived by the acceleration magnitude signal), and (maximum and standard deviation based on the acceleration magnitude signal)

100% classification accuracy is likewise achieved within less than 0.01 seconds for the K-nearest neighbors machine learning algorithm.

7.5 Logistic Regression

A unique characteristic of the logistic regression machine learning algorithm is the ability to consider the broad scope of information presented by the data to elucidate the modifications to the distribution regarding the movement disorder [14]. Figure 7.5 demonstrates the **Classifier output** section of the Weka Explorer for logistic

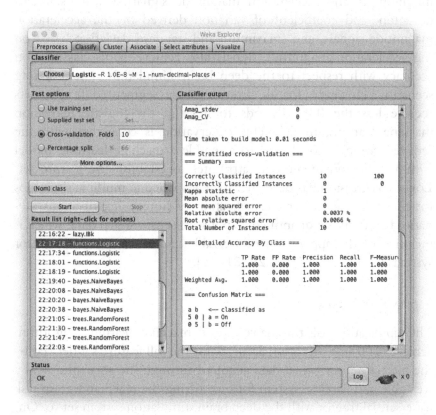

Fig. 7.5.   Logistic regression applying the full feature set for distinguishing deep brain stimulation system set to 'On' and 'Off' status regarding the reach and grasp task for essential tremor quantified by the smartphone as a wearable and wireless inertial sensor system.

regression with respect to the full feature set for machine learning classification applied to distinguish between essential tremor reach and grasp task for the deep brain stimulation system set to 'On' and 'Off' status. Using the smartphone as a wearable and wireless inertial sensor system to quantify the reach and grasp task for essential tremor with the deep brain stimulation system set to 'On' and 'Off' status logistic regression achieves 100% classification accuracy for distinguishing between the deep brain stimulation system setting scenarios. The logistic regression model requires 0.01 seconds to develop.

Consideration of the three segmented feature sets (maximum and minimum of the acceleration magnitude signal), (mean, standard deviation, and coefficient of variation derived by the acceleration magnitude signal), and (maximum and standard deviation based on the acceleration magnitude signal) also achieve 100% classification accuracy with respect to the deep brain stimulation system setting scenarios. However, for all three of these segmented feature sets require less the 0.01 seconds to develop the logistic regression machine learning model. This observation is consistent with the reduced computational load to assemble a machine learning model with a reduction in numeric attributes to establish the feature set. Logistic regression has been successfully applied in multiple situations for the machine learning classification of human health status scenarios based on the quantified response of sensor signal data, which is inclusive of the application of wearable and wireless inertial sensor systems [6–11, 14, 17, 26, 29, 31–34].

7.6 Naïve Bayes

The application of the naïve Bayes machine learning algorithm achieves 100% classification accuracy for the full feature set derived by the inertial sensor signal data acquired through the smartphone as a wearable and wireless system for quantifying the reach and grasp task for essential tremor with the deep brain stimulation system set to 'On' and 'Off' status. The time to develop the naïve Bayes machine learning model is less than 0.01 seconds. Figure 7.6 summarizes the

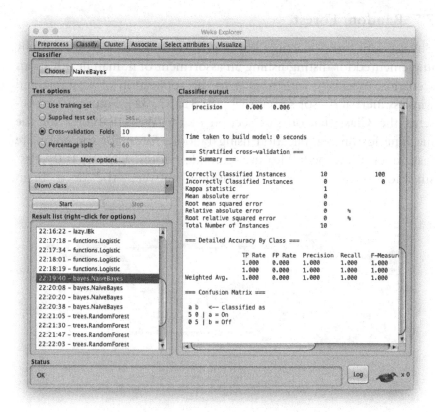

Fig. 7.6. Naïve Bayes with respect to the full feature set for distinguishing between deep brain stimulation system set to 'On' and 'Off' status for essential tremor using the reach and grasp task, which is quantified using a smartphone as a wearable and wireless inertial sensor system.

Classifier output section of the Weka Explorer for the machine learning application involving naïve Bayes. With regard to the segmented feature sets (maximum and minimum of the acceleration magnitude signal), (mean, standard deviation, and coefficient of variation derived by the acceleration magnitude signal), and (maximum and standard deviation based on the acceleration magnitude signal) 100% classification accuracy is also achieved in less than 0.01 seconds.

7.7 Random Forest

The random forest machine learning algorithm has been successfully implemented for distinguishing an assortment of human health status scenarios, especially with respect to the application of wearable and wireless inertial sensor systems [9, 29, 31, 32, 34]. Figure 7.7 represents the **Classifier output** section of the Weka Explorer for the machine learning application using random forest for the complete feature set. With the full feature set random forest achieves 100% classification accuracy for distinguishing between the deep brain

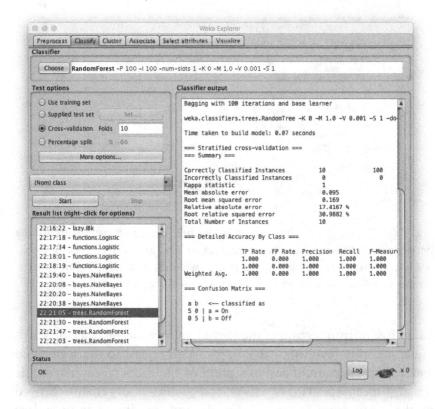

Fig. 7.7. Random forest applying the full feature set for differentiating with respect to deep brain stimulation system set to 'On' and 'Off' status for essential tremor using the reach and grasp task, which is quantified using a smartphone as a wearable and wireless inertial sensor system.

stimulation system set to 'On' and 'Off' for the essential tremor reach and grasp task, and the random forest machine learning model is generated within 0.07 seconds.

With respect to the segmented feature sets, two segmented feature sets (maximum and minimum of the acceleration magnitude signal and maximum and standard deviation based on the acceleration magnitude signal) achieve 90% classification accuracy. One instance of deep brain stimulation system set to 'On' is misclassified as deep brain stimulation system set to 'Off'. Both of these segmented feature sets require 0.02 seconds to develop the random forest machine learning model.

By contrast the segmented feature set composed of the mean, standard deviation, and coefficient of variation derived by the acceleration magnitude signal achieves 100% classification accuracy with random forest. The time to develop the random forest machine learning model is reduced to only 0.02 seconds, which constitutes a three-and-a half times reduction relative to the random forest machine learning model utilizing the full feature set. This finding of the opportunity to reduce processing time while maintaining the classification accuracy performance underscores the utility of investigating segmented feature sets relative to the original full feature set.

7.8 Multilayer Perceptron Neural Network

The multilayer perceptron neural network featured in WEKA has been applied to the differentiation of numerous human health status scenarios that have prevalently applied wearable and wireless inertial sensor systems [6–12, 18, 20–25, 27–32, 34–36]. Figure 7.8 presents the **Classifier output** section of the Weka Explorer for the multilayer perceptron neural network while applying the complete feature set. The multilayer perceptron neural network attains 100% classification accuracy and requires 0.09 seconds to develop the machine learning model. Figure 7.9 features the derived multilayer perceptron neural network, which is comprised of five input layers, three hidden layers, and two output layers.

The three segmented feature sets (maximum and minimum of the acceleration magnitude signal), (mean, standard deviation, and

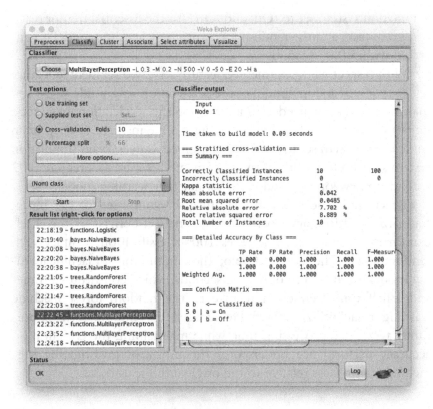

Fig. 7.8. Multilayer perceptron neural network based on the complete feature set for distinguishing deep brain stimulation system set to 'On' and 'Off' status for essential tremor using the reach and grasp task that is quantified by a wearable and wireless inertial sensor system represented by a smartphone.

coefficient of variation derived by the acceleration magnitude signal), and (maximum and standard deviation based on the acceleration magnitude signal) also attain 100% classification accuracy for distinguishing the deep brain stimulation system set to 'On' and 'Off' status. However, the time to develop the multilayer perceptron neural network is reduced to 0.01 seconds. The reduction in the number of numeric attributes for the multilayer perceptron neural network decreases the machine learning development time by a factor of nine.

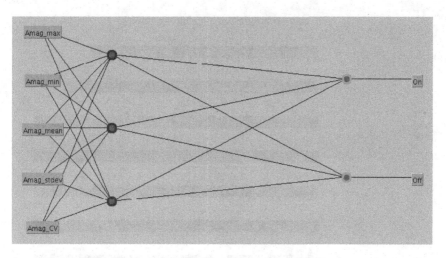

Fig. 7.9. Multilayer perceptron neural network derived for classifying two output layers through incorporating five input layers and three hidden layers.

7.9 Consideration of Most Appropriate Machine Learning Algorithms

With the performance capabilities of the seven respective machine learning algorithms addressed, the process of selecting the most appropriate algorithms is conducted in consideration of the complete feature set. The two significant performance parameters for the machine learning algorithms are the classification accuracy and time to develop the machine learning classification model. As previously established, the performance parameters are sequentially organized with primary emphasis toward the classification accuracy and secondary focus toward the time to establish the machine learning classification model [9, 11, 12, 29, 31, 34, 35].

The two performance parameters of the seven selected machine learning algorithms (support vector machine, J48 decision tree, K-nearest neighbors, logistic regression, naïve Bayes, random forest, and multilayer perceptron neural network) are visually organized in graphical form. Figure 7.10 represents classification accuracy achieved for distinguishing between the deep brain stimulation system set to

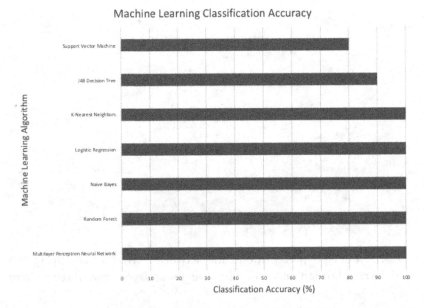

Fig. 7.10. Classification accuracy for differentiating the deep brain stimulation system set to 'On' and 'Off' status for the essential tremor reach and grasp task with quantified signal data provided by a smartphone functioning as a wearable and wireless system for seven machine learning algorithms (support vector machine, J48 decision tree, K-nearest neighbors, logistic regression, naïve Bayes, random forest, and multilayer perceptron neural network).

'On' and 'Off' for the essential tremor reach and grasp task using the quantified signal data acquired by the smartphone representing a wearable and wireless system. Figure 7.11 displays the time to develop the respective machine learning models.

Five of the machine learning classification algorithms achieve 100% classification accuracy with respect to the complete feature set:

- K-nearest neighbors
- Logistic regression
- Naïve Bayes

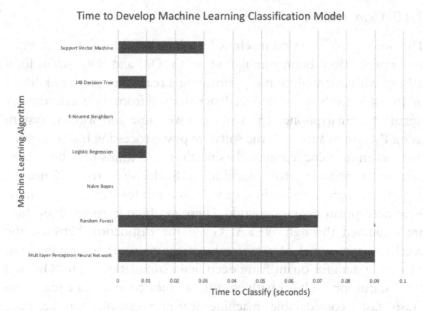

Fig. 7.11. Time to develop the respective machine learning models for the seven selected machine learning algorithms (support vector machine, J48 decision tree, K-nearest neighbors, logistic regression, naïve Bayes, random forest, and multilayer perceptron neural network). Note that the K-nearest neighbors and naïve Bayes require less than 0.01 seconds to develop their respective machine learning algorithms.

- Random forest
- Multilayer perceptron neural network

Of these five machine learning algorithms, the K-nearest neighbors and naïve Bayes demonstrate the ability to develop their machine learning models in less than 0.01 seconds. Therefore, based on the primary performance parameter of classification accuracy and secondary performance parameter of time to develop the machine learning model, the K-nearest neighbors and naïve Bayes machine learning algorithms provided by WEKA demonstrate the optimal performance.

7.10 Conclusion

The objective of applying machine learning classification to differentiate between deep brain stimulation set to 'On' and 'Off' status for a subject with essential tremor performing a reach and grasp task based on the objectively quantified feedback derived from the accelerometer signal of a smartphone representing a wearable and wireless system using Python to automate the software post-processing has been satisfied. Seven machine learning classification algorithms have been considered: support vector machine, J48 decision tree, K-nearest neighbors, logistic regression, naïve Bayes, random forest, and multilayer perceptron neural network. These machine learning algorithms are evaluated through WEKA. Given the distinction between the accelerometer signal of a smartphone representing a wearable and wireless system for quantifying deep brain stimulation set to 'On' and 'Off' status for a subject with essential tremor conducting a reach and grasp task, considerable machine learning classification accuracy within reasonable time constraints is attained. K-nearest neighbors and naïve Bayes provide the optimal performance in terms of classification accuracy and time to develop the machine learning model.

The process for satisfying the objective has been achieved through the sequential and evolutionary process. In Chapter 2, 'General Concept of Preliminary Network Centric Therapy Applying Deep Brain Stimulation for Ameliorating Movement Disorders with Machine Learning Classification using Python Based on Feedback from a Smartphone as a Wearable and Wireless System' the preliminary aspects for satisfying the objective are considered. A description of essential tremor, the reach and grasp task, deep brain stimulation, the smartphone for providing inertial sensor signal quantification as a wearable and wireless system, WEKA for machine learning classification, and the application of Python to post-process the accelerometer signal data are presented.

The software development process is discussed in Chapter 3 'Global Algorithm Development'. Requirements and pseudo code are established for the automated post-processing of the acquired accelerometer signal data. As the software development process evolves

Python is selected as the most appropriate programming language. The opportunity for continuous improvement, which is known as Kaizen, is addressed.

In Chapter 4 'Incremental Software Development using Python' the requirements and pseudo code are interleaved. A preliminary version of the software program using Python using the Jupyter Notebook is presented with testing and evaluation. With the identification of an anomaly in the accelerometer signal identified, an amendment to the software program using Python through interpolation of the signal data is presented.

A fully automated version of the Python software program using the Jupyter Notebook is achieved in Chapter 5 'Automation of Feature Set Extraction using Python'. The Python software program is progressively evolved to enable the automated post-processing of the entire accelerometer signal data acquired by the smartphone functioning as a wearable and wireless system. The post-processing of the accelerometer signal data for the deep brain stimulation set to 'On' and 'Off' is conducted within the developed Python software program.

Subsequently, the seven machine learning algorithms available through the WEKA are described in Chapter 6 'Waikato Environment for Knowledge Analysis (WEKA) a Perspective Consideration of Multiple Machine Learning Classification Algorithms and Applications'. These seven machine learning algorithms are support vector machine, J48 decision tree, K-nearest neighbors, logistic regression, naïve Bayes, random forest, and multilayer perceptron neural network. The processes for conducting these seven machine learning algorithms provided by WEKA are demonstrated, and the function principles of these seven machine learning algorithms are described.

Chapter 7 'Machine Learning Classification of Essential Tremor using a Reach and Grasp Task with Deep Brain Stimulation System Set to 'On' and 'Off' Status', emphasizes output resultant of machine learning classification through the WEKA. Seven machine learning algorithms are considered: support vector machine, J48 decision tree, K-nearest neighbors, logistic regression, naïve Bayes, random forest, and multilayer perceptron neural network. Two performance parameters were evaluated for the respective machine learning algorithms. Primary focus emphasized classification accuracy and secondary focus pertained to time to develop the machine learning model. In conclusion, K-nearest neighbors and naïve Bayes demonstrated the optimal performance.

In Chapter 8, 'Advanced Concepts' consists of a perspective of multiple primary subjects of future significance. The advent of the conformal wearable and wireless inertial sensor system constitutes a significant development for the evolution of Network Centric Therapy. Network Centric Therapy incorporates the amalgamation of wearable and wireless inertial sensor systems with connectivity to Cloud computing resources and machine learning for augmenting clinical acuity. Network Centric Therapy has recently evolved to the domain of deep learning.

References

1. LeMoyne, R., Tomycz, N., Mastroianni, T., McCandless, C., Cozza, M. and Peduto, D. (2015). Implementation of a smartphone wireless accelerometer platform for establishing deep brain stimulation treatment efficacy of essential tremor with machine learning, *Proc. 37th Annual International Conference of the IEEE, Engineering in Medicine and Biology Society (EMBS)*, pp. 6772–6775.
2. LeMoyne, R., Coroian, C., Mastroianni, T., Opalinski, P., Cozza, M. and Grundfest W. (2009). *Biomedical Engineering*, ed. Barros de Mello, C. A., Chapter 10 "The Merits of Artificial Proprioception, with Applications in Biofeedback Gait Rehabilitation Concepts and Movement Disorder Characterization," (InTech, Vienna), pp. 165–198.
3. LeMoyne, R. and Mastroianni, T. (2015). *Mobile Health Technologies, Methods and Protocols*, eds. Rasooly, A. and Herold, K. E., Chapter 23 "Use of Smartphones and Portable Media Devices for Quantifying Human Movement Characteristics of Gait, Tendon Reflex Response, and Parkinson's Disease Hand Tremor," (Springer, New York) pp. 335–358.
4. LeMoyne, R. and Mastroianni, T. (2016). *Telemedicine*, "Telemedicine Perspectives for Wearable and Wireless Applications Serving the Domain

of Neurorehabilitation and Movement Disorder Treatment," (SMGroup, Dover) pp. 1–10.

5. LeMoyne, R. and Mastroianni, T. (2017). *Wireless MEMS Networks and Applications*, ed. Uttamchandani, D., Chapter 6 "Wearable and Wireless Gait Analysis Platforms: Smartphones and Portable Media Devices," (Elsevier, New York) pp. 129–152.

6. LeMoyne, R. and Mastroianni, T. (2017). *Smartphones from an Applied Research Perspective*, ed. Mohamudally, N., Chapter 1 "Smartphone and Portable Media Device: A Novel Pathway toward the Diagnostic Characterization of Human Movement," (InTech, Rijeka) pp. 1–24.

7. LeMoyne, R. and Mastroianni, T. (2018). *Wearable and Wireless Systems for Healthcare I: Gait and Reflex Response Quantification*, (Springer, Singapore).

8. LeMoyne, R. and Mastroianni, T. (2018). *Wearable and Wireless Systems for Healthcare I: Gait and Reflex Response Quantification*, Chapter 9 "Role of Machine Learning for Gait and Reflex Response Classification," (Springer, Singapore) pp. 111–120.

9. LeMoyne, R., Mastroianni, T., Whiting, D. and Tomycz, N. (2019). *Wearable and Wireless Systems for Healthcare II: Movement Disorder Evaluation and Deep Brain Stimulation Systems*, (Springer, Singapore).

10. LeMoyne, R., Mastroianni, T., Whiting, D. and Tomycz, N. (2019). *Wearable and Wireless Systems for Healthcare II: Movement Disorder Evaluation and Deep Brain Stimulation Systems*, Chapter 8 "Role of Machine Learning for Classification of Movement Disorder and Deep Brain Stimulation Status," (Springer, Singapore) pp. 99–111.

11. LeMoyne, R. and Mastroianni, T. (2019). *Smartphones: Recent Innovations and Applications*, ed. Dabove, P., Chapter 7 "Network Centric Therapy for Wearable and Wireless Systems," (Nova Science Publishers, Hauppauge).

12. LeMoyne, R. and Mastroianni, T. (2020). *Multilayer Perceptrons: Theory and Applications*, ed. Vang-Mata, R., Chapter 2 "Machine Learning Classification for Network Centric Therapy Utilizing the Multilayer Perceptron Neural Network," (Nova Science Publishers, Hauppauge) pp. 39–76.

13. LeMoyne, R., Kerr, W., Zanjani, K. and Mastroianni, T. (2014). Implementation of an iPod wireless accelerometer application using

machine learning to classify disparity of hemiplegic and healthy patellar tendon reflex pair, *J. Med. Imaging Health Inform.*, 4, pp. 21–28.

14. LeMoyne, R., Kerr, W., Mastroianni, T. and Hessel, A. (2014). Implementation of machine learning for classifying hemiplegic gait disparity through use of a force plate, *Proc. 13th International Conference on Machine Learning and Applications (ICMLA), IEEE*, pp. 379–382.

15. LeMoyne, R., Mastroianni, T., Hessel, A. and Nishikawa, K. (2015). Implementation of machine learning for classifying prosthesis type through conventional gait analysis, *Proc. 37th Annual International Conference of the IEEE, Engineering in Medicine and Biology Society (EMBS)*, pp. 202–205.

16. LeMoyne, R. and Mastroianni, T. (2015). Machine learning classification of a hemiplegic and healthy patellar tendon reflex pair through an iPod wireless gyroscope platform, *Proc. 45th Society for Neuroscience Annual Meeting*.

17. LeMoyne, R., Kerr, W. and Mastroianni, T. (2015). Implementation of machine learning with an iPod application mounted to cane for classifying assistive device usage, *J. Med. Imaging Health Inform.*, 5, pp. 1404–1408.

18. LeMoyne, R., Mastroianni, T., Hessel, A. and Nishikawa, K. (2015). Application of a multilayer perceptron neural network for classifying software platforms of a powered prosthesis through a force plate, *Proc. 14th International Conference on Machine Learning and Applications (ICMLA), IEEE*, pp. 402–405.

19. LeMoyne, R., Mastroianni, T., Hessel, A. and Nishikawa, K. (2015). Ankle rehabilitation system with feedback from a smartphone wireless gyroscope platform and machine learning classification, *Proc. 14th International Conference on Machine Learning and Applications (ICMLA), IEEE*, pp. 406–409.

20. LeMoyne, R., Heerinckx, F., Aranca, T., De Jager, R., Zesiewicz, T. and Saal, H. J. (2016). Wearable body and wireless inertial sensors for machine learning classification of gait for people with Friedreich's ataxia, *Proc. 13th Annual International Body Sensor Networks Conference (BSN), IEEE*, pp. 147–151.

21. LeMoyne, R. and Mastroianni, T. (2016). Implementation of a smartphone as a wireless gyroscope platform for quantifying reduced arm swing in hemiplegic gait with machine learning classification by

multilayer perceptron neural network, *Proc. 38th Annual International Conference of the IEEE, Engineering in Medicine and Biology Society (EMBS)*, pp. 2626–2630.

22. LeMoyne, R. and Mastroianni, T. (2016). Smartphone wireless gyroscope platform for machine learning classification of hemiplegic patellar tendon reflex pair disparity through a multilayer perceptron neural network, *Proc. Wireless Health (WH), IEEE*, pp. 1–6.

23. LeMoyne, R. and Mastroianni, T. (2016). Implementation of a multilayer perceptron neural network for classifying a hemiplegic and healthy reflex pair using an iPod wireless gyroscope platform, *Proc. 46th Society for Neuroscience Annual Meeting.*

24. LeMoyne, R. and Mastroianni, T. (2017). Virtual Proprioception for eccentric training, *Proc. 39th Annual International Conference of the IEEE, Engineering in Medicine and Biology Society (EMBS)*, pp. 4557–4561.

25. LeMoyne, R. and Mastroianni, T. (2017). Wireless gyroscope platform enabled by a portable media device for quantifying wobble board therapy, *Proc. 39th Annual International Conference of the IEEE, Engineering in Medicine and Biology Society (EMBS)*, pp. 2662–2666.

26. LeMoyne, R. and Mastroianni, T. (2017). Implementation of a smartphone wireless gyroscope platform with machine learning for classifying disparity of a hemiplegic patellar tendon reflex pair, *J. Mech. Med. Biol.*, 17, 1750083.

27. LeMoyne, R., Mastroianni, T., Tomycz, N., Whiting, D., Oh, M., McCandless, C., Currivan, C. and Peduto, D. (2017). Implementation of a multilayer perceptron neural network for classifying deep brain stimulation in 'On' and 'Off' modes through a smartphone representing a wearable and wireless sensor application, *Proc. 47th Society for Neuroscience Annual Meeting, Featured in Hot Topics (Top 1% of Abstracts).*

28. LeMoyne, R., Mastroianni, T., McCandless, C., Currivan, C., Whiting, D. and Tomycz, N. (2018). Implementation of a smartphone as a wearable and wireless accelerometer and gyroscope platform for ascertaining deep brain stimulation treatment efficacy of Parkinson's disease through machine learning classification, *Adv. Park. Dis.*, 7, pp. 19–30.

29. LeMoyne, R., Mastroianni, T., McCandless, C., Currivan, C., Whiting, D. and Tomycz, N. (2018). Implementation of a smartphone as a

wearable and wireless inertial sensor platform for determining efficacy of deep brain stimulation for Parkinson's disease tremor through machine learning, *Proc. 48th Society for Neuroscience Annual Meeting, Nanosymposium.*

30. LeMoyne, R. and Mastroianni, T. (2018). Implementation of a smartphone as a wearable and wireless gyroscope platform for machine learning classification of hemiplegic gait through a multilayer perceptron neural network, *Proc. 17th International Conference on Machine Learning and Applications (ICMLA), IEEE*, pp. 946–950.

31. LeMoyne, R., Mastroianni, T., Whiting, D. and Tomycz, N. (2019). *Wearable and Wireless Systems for Healthcare II: Movement Disorder Evaluation and Deep Brain Stimulation Systems*, Chapter 9 "Assessment of Machine Learning Classification Strategies for the Differentiation of Deep Brain Stimulation "On" and "Off" Status for Parkinson's Disease Using a Smartphone as a Wearable and Wireless Inertial Sensor for Quantified Feedback," (Springer, Singapore) pp. 113–126.

32. LeMoyne, R., Mastroianni, T., McCandless, C., Whiting, D. and Tomycz, N. (2019). Evaluation of machine learning algorithms for classifying deep brain stimulation respective of 'On' and 'Off' status, *Proc. 9th International IEEE Conference on Neural Engineering (NER), IEEE/EMBS*, pp. 483–488.

33. LeMoyne, R. and Mastroianni, T. (2019). Classification of software control architectures for a powered prosthesis through conventional gait analysis using machine learning applications, *J. Mech. Med. Biol.*, 19, 1950044.

34. LeMoyne, R., Mastroianni, T., Whiting, D. and Tomycz, N. (2019). Network Centric Therapy for deep brain stimulation status parametric analysis with machine learning classification, *Proc. 49th Society for Neuroscience Annual Meeting, Nanosymposium.*

35. LeMoyne, R., Mastroianni, T., Whiting, D. and Tomycz, N. (2019). Preliminary Network Centric Therapy for machine learning classification of deep brain stimulation status for the treatment of Parkinson's disease with a conformal wearable and wireless inertial sensor, *Adv. Park. Dis.*, 8, pp. 75–91.

36. Mastroianni, T. and LeMoyne, R. (2016). Application of a multilayer perceptron neural network with an iPod as a wireless gyroscope platform

to classify reduced arm swing gait for people with Erb's palsy, *Proc. 46th Society for Neuroscience Annual Meeting.*

37. Hall, M., Frank, E., Holmes, G., Pfahringer, B., Reutemann, P. and Witten I. H. (2009). The WEKA data mining software: An update, *ACM SIGKDD Explor. Newsl.*, 11, pp. 10–18.

38. Witten, I. H., Frank, E. and Hall, M. A. (2011). *Data Mining: Practical Machine Learning Tools and Techniques*, 3rd Ed. (Morgan Kaufmann Publishers, Burlington).

39. WEKA [http://www.cs.waikato.ac.nz/~ml/weka]

Chapter 8

Advanced Concepts

8.1 Introduction

Multiple advanced concepts warrant consideration for the progressive evolution of Network Centric Therapy for the treatment of movement disorders. Recent developments have enabled the incorporation of conformal wearable and wireless inertial sensor systems for the quantification of a movement disorder, such as Parkinson's disease, response to an assortment of deep brain stimulation parameter configurations [1–5]. An additional extrapolation of the capabilities of Network Centric Therapy beyond the constraints of machine learning involves the incorporation of deep learning, such as the convolutional neural network. Deep learning incorporating TensorFlow has been successfully applied to distinguish an assortment of deep brain stimulation parameter configurations for treating movement disorders, such as Parkinson's disease [6, 7].

8.2 Conformal Wearable and Wireless Inertial Sensor System for Quantifying Movement Disorder Response to an Assortment of Deep Brain Stimulation Parameter Configurations with Machine Learning

Movement disorders, such as essential tremor and Parkinson's disease, involve distinct characteristics of tremor that have been successfully quantified through wearable and wireless inertial sensor systems, such as the smartphone, with successful differentiation of response to deep brain stimulation parameter configuration scenarios through machine learning [8–18]. The conformal wearable and wireless inertial sensor system, such as the BioStamp nPoint, constitutes a considerable advance for the quantification of movement disorder tremor characteristics. The BioStamp nPoint conformally mounts about the human anatomy, such as the dorsum of the hand, by adhesive medium. The mass of the BioStamp nPoint is less than 10 grams, and the profile is comparable to a bandage [1–5, 19]. Figure 8.1 presents the associated apparatus for the BioStamp nPoint, and Figure 8.2 provides a representation of the mounting of the BioStamp nPoint about the dorsum of the hand.

The segmented wireless connectivity features of the BioStamp nPoint constitute a paradigm shift. Local wireless operation of the BioStamp nPoint conformal wearable and wireless inertial sensor system is achieved by connectivity to a tablet. Access to a secure Cloud computing environment is achieved through wireless connectivity enabled through a smartphone [1–5, 19].

Fig. 8.1. The BioStamp nPoint conformal wearable and wireless inertial sensor system, docking station, smartphone, and tablet.

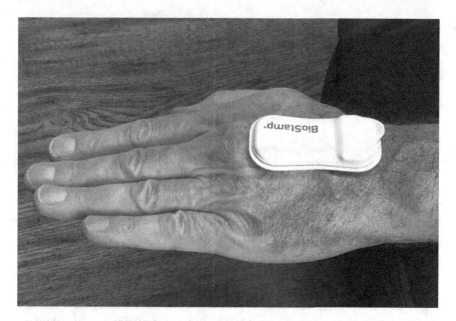

Fig. 8.2.   Mounting of the BioStamp nPoint about the dorsum of the hand for the quantification of movement disorder tremor.

For a subject with Parkinson's disease, multiple deep brain stimulation parameter settings, such as amplitude set to 4.0 mA, 2.5 mA, 1.0 mA, and 'Off' status representing a baseline, were evaluated. The BioStamp nPoint conformal wearable and wireless inertial sensor system was mounted about the dorsum of the hand and quantified the respective Parkinson's disease hand tremor response. Using a similar technique relative to Chapters 3 to 5, Python was incorporated to post-process the inertial sensor signal data to a feature set amenable for the Attribute-Relation File Format (ARFF) for machine learning classification incorporating the Waikato Environment for Knowledge Analysis (WEKA). The acceleration magnitude signal response to the deep brain stimulation amplitude settings (4.0 mA, 2.5 mA, 1.0 mA, and 'Off' status representing a baseline) are presented in Figures 8.3 through 8.6. An assortment of machine learning classification algorithms, such as the multilayer perceptron neural network, J48 decision tree, K-nearest neighbors, support vector machine, logistic regression, and random forest, achieved

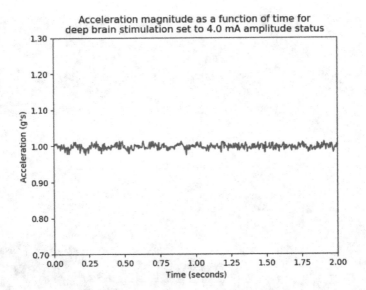

Fig. 8.3.   Deep brain stimulation (amplitude set to 4.0 mA) for a subject with Parkinson's disease quantified by the BioStamp nPoint conformal wearable and wireless inertial sensor system [1, 2, 4, 5].

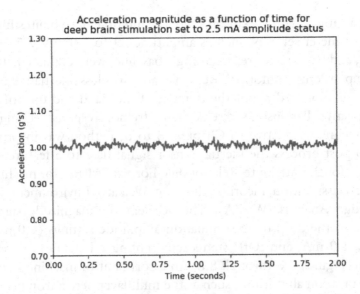

Fig. 8.4.   Deep brain stimulation (amplitude set to 2.5 mA) for a subject with Parkinson's disease quantified by the BioStamp nPoint conformal wearable and wireless inertial sensor system [1, 2, 4, 5].

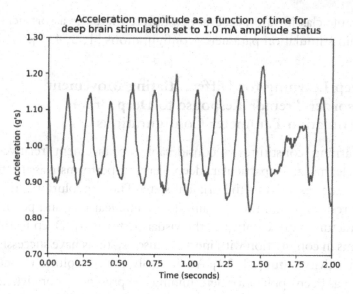

Fig. 8.5. Deep brain stimulation (amplitude set to 1.0 mA) for a subject with Parkinson's disease quantified by the BioStamp nPoint conformal wearable and wireless inertial sensor system [1, 2, 4, 5].

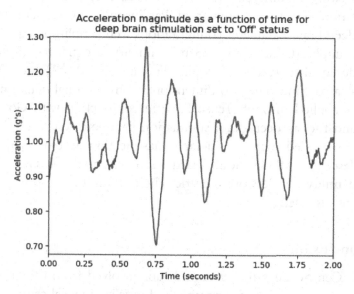

Fig. 8.6. Deep brain stimulation (set to 'Off' status) for a subject with Parkinson's disease quantified by the BioStamp nPoint conformal wearable and wireless inertial sensor system [1, 2, 4, 5].

considerable classification accuracy to differentiate the assortment of deep brain stimulation parameter configurations [1, 2, 4, 5].

8.3 Deep Learning for Differentiating Movement Disorder Tremor Response to Deep Brain Stimulation Parameter Configurations

Deep learning constitutes a considerable advancement relative to machine learning. In particular, deep learning performs classification with the data reserved to the original state. The convolutional neural network resides within the domain of machine learning and possesses an architecture representative of the visual cortex [20]. Deep learning algorithms in conjunction with inertial sensor systems have successfully classified activity status [21–23]. Additionally, the convolutional neural network has been applied for determining the presence of bradykinesia for Parkinson's disease subjects based on inertial sensor data [24].

The BioStamp nPoint conformal wearable and wireless inertial sensor system was amalgamated with the deep learning convolutional neural network to differentiate six prescribed deep brain parameter configurations for the treatment of Parkinson's disease. The prescribed deep brain parameter configurations were amplitude equal to 4.0 mA, amplitude equal to 3.25 mA, amplitude equal to 2.5 mA, amplitude equal to 1.75 mA, amplitude equal to 1.0 mA, and 'Off' setting as a baseline. The two-dimensional convolutional neural network was applied through TensorFlow in conjunction with Google Colab, and the six deep brain stimulation parameter configurations were distinguished with considerable classification accuracy [6, 7]. The coalescence of these Cloud-based resources underscores the considerable utility of Network Centric Therapy for the treatment of movement disorders.

8.4 Conclusion

Network Centric Therapy has considerably evolved from the origins of applying smartphones as wearable and wireless inertial sensor systems with Internet connectivity to email resources as provisional

Cloud computing environments. The advent of conformal wearable and wireless inertial sensor systems, such as the BioStamp nPoint, offer notable utility for the quantification of movement disorders symptoms, and quantified response can be acquired with respect to an assortment of deep brain stimulation parameter configurations. Using similar techniques established in Chapters 3 to 5 regarding Python, the inertial sensor signal data was consolidated to a feature set for machine learning classification using WEKA while attaining considerable classification accuracy. Furthermore, deep learning incorporating a convolutional neural network has achieved considerable classification accuracy for differentiating more discretized deep brain stimulation parameter configurations for treating Parkinson's disease by contrast to conventional machine learning algorithms. Additionally, the deep learning classification was realized through Cloud computing resources, such as Google Colab featuring TensorFlow. These advanced concepts further imply the potential of Network Centric Therapy for the treatment of movement disorders as a representation of the Internet of Things for the domain of healthcare and the biomedical industry.

References

1. LeMoyne, R., Mastroianni, T., Whiting, D. and Tomycz, N. (2019). Network Centric Therapy for deep brain stimulation status parametric analysis with machine learning classification, *Proc. 49th Society for Neuroscience Annual Meeting, Nanosymposium.*

2. LeMoyne, R., Mastroianni, T., Whiting, D. and Tomycz, N. (2019). Preliminary Network Centric Therapy for machine learning classification of deep brain stimulation status for the treatment of Parkinson's disease with a conformal wearable and wireless inertial sensor, *Adv. Park. Dis.,* 8, pp. 75–91.

3. LeMoyne, R. and Mastroianni, T. (2020). *Multilayer Perceptrons: Theory and Applications,* ed. Vang-Mata, R., Chapter 2 "Machine Learning Classification for Network Centric Therapy Utilizing the Multilayer Perceptron Neural Network," (Nova Science Publishers, Hauppauge) pp. 39–76.

4. LeMoyne, R., Mastroianni, T., Whiting, D. and Tomycz, N. (2020). Parametric evaluation of deep brain stimulation parameter configurations for Parkinson's disease using a conformal wearable and wireless inertial sensor system and machine learning, *Proc. 42nd Annual International Conference of the IEEE, Engineering in Medicine and Biology Society (EMBS)*, pp. 3606–3611.

5. LeMoyne, R., Mastroianni, T., Whiting, D. and Tomycz, N. (2020). Distinction of an assortment of deep brain stimulation parameter configurations for treating Parkinson's disease using machine learning with quantification of tremor response through a conformal wearable and wireless inertial sensor, *Adv. Park. Dis.*, 9, pp. 21–39.

6. LeMoyne, R., Mastroianni, T., Whiting, D. and Tomycz, N. (2020). Application of deep learning to distinguish multiple deep brain stimulation parameter configurations for the treatment of Parkinson's disease, *Proc. 19th International Conference on Machine Learning and Applications (ICMLA), IEEE*, pp. 1106–1111.

7. LeMoyne, R., Mastroianni, T., Whiting, D. and Tomycz, N. (2021). Deep learning for differentiating parameter configurations of deep brain stimulation for treating Parkinson's disease incorporating conformal wearable and wireless inertial sensors as an evolution for Network Centric Therapy, *Proc. Society for Neuroscience Global Connectome: A Virtual Event*.

8. LeMoyne, R., Mastroianni, T., Whiting, D. and Tomycz, N. (2019). *Wearable and Wireless Systems for Healthcare II: Movement Disorder Evaluation and Deep Brain Stimulation Systems*, (Springer, Singapore).

9. LeMoyne, R., Mastroianni, T., Whiting, D. and Tomycz, N. (2019). *Wearable and Wireless Systems for Healthcare II: Movement Disorder Evaluation and Deep Brain Stimulation Systems*, Chapter 2 "Movement Disorders: Parkinson's Disease and Essential Tremor — A General Perspective," (Springer, Singapore) pp. 17–24.

10. LeMoyne, R., Mastroianni, T., Whiting, D. and Tomycz, N. (2019). *Wearable and Wireless Systems for Healthcare II: Movement Disorder Evaluation and Deep Brain Stimulation Systems*, Chapter 8 "Role of Machine Learning for Classification of Movement Disorder and Deep Brain Stimulation Status," (Springer, Singapore) pp. 99–111.

11. LeMoyne, R. and Mastroianni, T. (2019). *Smartphones: Recent Innovations and Applications,* ed. Dabove, P., Chapter 7 "Network Centric Therapy for Wearable and Wireless Systems," (Nova Science Publishers, Hauppauge).

12. LeMoyne, R., Tomycz, N., Mastroianni, T., McCandless, C., Cozza, M. and Peduto, D. (2015). Implementation of a smartphone wireless accelerometer platform for establishing deep brain stimulation treatment efficacy of essential tremor with machine learning, *Proc. 37th Annual International Conference of the IEEE, Engineering in Medicine and Biology Society (EMBS),* pp. 6772–6775.

13. LeMoyne, R. and Mastroianni, T. (2017). *Smartphones from an Applied Research Perspective,* ed. Mohamudally, N., Chapter 1 "Smartphone and Portable Media Device: A Novel Pathway Toward the Diagnostic Characterization of Human Movement," (InTech, Rijeka), pp. 1–24.

14. LeMoyne, R., Mastroianni, T., Tomycz, N., Whiting, D., Oh, M., McCandless, C., Currivan, C. and Peduto, D. (2017). Implementation of a multilayer perceptron neural network for classifying deep brain stimulation in 'On' and 'Off' modes through a smartphone representing a wearable and wireless sensor application, *Proc. 47th Society for Neuroscience Annual Meeting, featured in Hot Topics (Top 1% of Abstracts).*

15. LeMoyne, R., Mastroianni, T., McCandless, C., Currivan, C., Whiting, D. and Tomycz, N. (2018). Implementation of a smartphone as a wearable and wireless accelerometer and gyroscope platform for ascertaining deep brain stimulation treatment efficacy of Parkinson's disease through machine learning classification, *Adv. Park. Dis.,* 7, pp. 19–30.

16. LeMoyne, R., Mastroianni, T., McCandless, C., Currivan, C., Whiting, D. and Tomycz, N. (2018). Implementation of a smartphone as a wearable and wireless inertial sensor platform for determining efficacy of deep brain stimulation for Parkinson's disease tremor through machine learning, *Proc. 48th Society for Neuroscience Annual Meeting, Nanosymposium.*

17. LeMoyne, R., Mastroianni, T., Whiting, D. and Tomycz, N. (2019). *Wearable and Wireless Systems for Healthcare II: Movement Disorder Evaluation and Deep Brain Stimulation Systems,* Chapter 9 "Assessment of Machine Learning Classification Strategies for the Differentiation of

Deep Brain Stimulation "On" and "Off" Status for Parkinson's Disease Using a Smartphone as a Wearable and Wireless Inertial Sensor for Quantified Feedback," (Springer, Singapore) pp. 113–126.

18. LeMoyne, R., Mastroianni, T., McCandless, C., Whiting, D. and Tomycz, N. (2019). Evaluation of machine learning algorithms for classifying deep brain stimulation respective of 'On' and 'Off' status, *Proc. 9th International IEEE Conference on Neural Engineering (NER), IEEE/EMBS*, pp. 483–488.

19. MC10 Inc. [www.mc10inc.com/our-products#biostamp-npoint]

20. LeCun, Y., Bengio, Y. and Hinton G. (2015). Deep learning, *Nature*, 521, pp. 436–444.

21. Nweke, H. F., The, Y. W., Al-Garadi, M. A. and Alo, U. R. (2018). Deep learning algorithms for human activity recognition using mobile and wearable sensor networks: State of the art and research challenges, *Expert Syst. Appl.*, 105, pp. 233–261.

22. Zebin, T., Scully, P. J. and Ozanyan, K. B. (2016). Human activity recognition with inertial sensors using a deep learning approach, *Proc. IEEE Sensors*, pp. 1–3.

23. Ha, S. and Choi, S. (2016). Convolutional neural networks for human activity recognition using multiple accelerometer and gyroscope sensors, *Proc. 2016 International Joint Conference Neural Networks (IJCNN), IEEE*, pp. 381–388.

24. Eskofier, B. M., Lee, S. I., Daneault, J. F., Golabchi, F. N., Ferreira-Carvalho, G., Vergara-Diaz, G., Sapienza, S., Costante, G., Klucken, J., Kautz, T. and Bonato, P. (2016). Recent machine learning advancements in sensor-based mobility analysis: Deep learning for Parkinson's disease assessment, *Proc. 38th Annual International Conference of the IEEE, Engineering in Medicine and Biology Society (EMBS)*, pp. 655–658.

Index